FACING DEPRESSION

Exploring its Cause and Cure

By
William J. Finnigan, D. Min.

Facing Depressions, Exploring its Cause and Cure
©William J. Finnigan, D. Min.
November 2018
Printed in the United States of America

ISBN: 978-1-7321746-4-1

> **Disclaimer**
>
> The author of this work has quoted the writers of many articles and books. This does not mean that the author endorses or recommends the works of others. If the author quotes someone, it does not mean that he agrees with all of the author's tenets, statements, concepts, or words, whether in the work quoted or any other work of the author. There has been no attempt to alter the meaning of the quotes; and therefore, some of the quotes are long in order to give the entire sense of the passage.

All rights reserved solely by the author. The author guarantees all contents are original and do not infringe upon the legal rights of any other person or work. No part of this book may be reproduced in any form without the permission of the author. The views expressed in this book are not necessarily those of the publisher.

Unless otherwise indicated, Bible quotations are taken from **The Holy Bible, Authorized King James Version**, 2003, Thomas Nelson, Inc., all rights reserved. This **Holy Bible** may be quoted or reprinted without prior written permission with the following qualifications: Up to and including 1,000 verses may be quoted in printed form if the verses quoted amount to less than 50 percent of a complete book of the **Bible** and make up less than 50 percent of the total work in which they are quoted. All **KJV** quotations must conform accurately to the **KJV** text.

Dr. Finnigan may be reached at:
8883 Sherwood Dr. NE
Warren, Ohio 44484
email:bilfinn1@yahoo.com

Formatting, Editing and Publishing Assistance By:
The Old Paths Publications, Inc.
Cleveland, Ga 30528
www.theoldpathspublications.com
email: TOP@theoldpathspublications.com

DEDICATION

To Justin--my beloved grandson

In your brief journey on this earth, you lived life to the full. You left us a legacy to follow, demonstrating the meaning of glorifying Christ—whether in life or in death.

TABLE OF CONTENTS

FACING DEPRESSION 1
DEDICATION 3
TABLE OF CONTENTS 5
FACING DEPRESSION 9
Exploring its Cause and Cure 9
    PROLOGUE 9
PART I 13
    SETTING THE STAGE 13
Chapter One: 15
    How Did We Get Here? 15
        Man: His God-given Purpose and Function 15
        Why Drugs? 16
Chapter Two 19
    The Early Stage of Depression 19
        Self-centeredness: Nothing New 20
        Little Things Unchecked Become Big 22
        It Happens to the Best 24
        Supernatural Provision 25
PART II 27
    SURFACE CAUSES OF DEPRESSION 27
Chapter Three 29
    Unfulfilled Goals 29
        Elijah's Disappointment 32
Chapter Four 35
    Losing Sight of God 35
        The Exodus from the Ministry 35
        Moses' Disillusionment 39
        Jeremiah's Mood Swings 42
        A Horrendous Test 46
Chapter Five 49
    Wrong Response to Trials 49
        Temptation or Trial—Which? 49
        Trials of the Faithful 50
        Despising Trials 53

       Fainting in Trial 54
       Endurance in Trial....................................... 55
Chapter Six 59
   Lack of Appreciation and Understanding from Others.. 59
       Moses' Problem 60
PART III 64
   ROOT CAUSES OF DEPRESSION 64
Chapter Seven 65
   Covetousness.. 65
       The Peril of Greed....................................... 65
       Asaph's Conflict 66
       The Wicked Described................................ 68
       A Radical Conclusion 70
       The Turning Point....................................... 70
       Hope Restored... 72
Chapter Eight 73
   Unbelief... 73
       A Matter of Life or Death 73
       The Garden of Eden 73
Chapter Nine 77
   Resentment toward God.................................. 77
       Cain's "Dis-ABEL-ment"............................ 77
       A Case of Divine Injustice? 77
Chapter Ten 81
   Hopelessness 81
PART IV 84
   THE REMEDY FOR DEPRESSION 84
Chapter Eleven.. 85
   Why Drugs Don't Work.................................. 85
       Drugs Cannot Reach the Root Problem....... 85
       Drugs May Be the Problem! 87
Chapter Twelve 93
   The Starting Point.. 93
Chapter Thirteen 97
   Coming to a Moment of Truth........................ 97

TABLE OF CONTENTS

       Prayerfully Taking Personal Responsibility 97
       A Renewed Mind 98
Chapter Fourteen.. 101
   Rehearsing God's Sovereignty............................. 101
Chapter Fifteen 103
   Understanding God's Purposes for Trial 103
       Trials Develop Patience and Endurance. ... 104
       Trials Validate our Sonship. 107
       Trials Generate Fervent Worship.............. 108
       Trials Equip Us for Ministry to Others. 112
       Trials Promote Christ-likeness.................. 114
       HIS DISCIPLE.. 116
Chapter Sixteen... 121
   Recognizing that No Problem Can Rob Your Joy OR RECOGNIZING YOUR IDENTITY IN CHRIST (Exchanged life?) 121
       Making Right Choices 122
       Preoccupation with Living for God's Glory
       125
EPILOGUE 131
   A PERSONAL TESTIMONY 131
Endnotes.. 133
A Summation and Glossary of Terms....................... 137
       Discouragement 138
       Depression.. 139
       Disclaimer 142
       Burnout 143
       Oppression 145
       A Lesson from Wildlife 146
       Addendum.. 147
Selected Bibliography 149
About the Author 151

FACING DEPRESSION
Exploring its Cause and Cure

PROLOGUE

Depression in America has reached **alarming** proportions! According to one source, it is estimated that nearly 19 million adults suffer from serious depression, which is almost 10% of the U.S. population. This does not include the millions of teenagers who are depressed and prone to suicide. The World Health Organization says that cases of depression are "doubling every ten years and will be, by 2020, the most pervasive illness in the world, ...second to heart disease, and the second major cause of death... In the US and Australia, and throughout the western world, a pall of stigma and secrecy still surrounds this experience."[1] Added to these figures are the multiplied millions who feel down, blue, and unhappy with their station in life, not to mention the astounding increase of depression among children.

What accounts for such an epidemic? How can this condition exist in a nation so blessed with opportunity and wealth? Unlike most of the world, our young people have been born with the proverbial silver spoon in their mouths, yet the suicide rate continues to surge. What's going on? Among other things, the breakdown of family life, along with an explosion of technology and "social media" has undoubtedly contributed to this precarious phenomenon. It's so easy for our youth to be totally absorbed in a "make believe" world via a hand-held computer! Obviously we are faced with an issue that needs to be seriously and squarely addressed.

It is significant that our culture, along with others in the world, is rapidly being overtaken by drug addiction of all sorts. Not only are we facing the illegal drug usage of cocaine, heroin, and the like, but also the legal prescription market of so-called psychotropic medication. The term "psychotropic" is derived from two words meaning "mind" (psycho) and "change" (tropic). These are drugs that alter or affect the mind, emotions and behavior. Products like Prozac, Paxil, Zoloft and Lexapro are escalating at an alarming rate in the treatment of depression. It is estimated that 300 million prescriptions for Prozac and anti-depressants are filled annually in the USA alone![2]

The tragedy is that whether legal or illegal, drugs only deal with symptoms, not the cause of the problem. There is no medical cure for depression. Yet precious people endure this condition with drug assistance, never realizing that depression can be cured. Therefore, the thrust of this book is to explore both the cause and cure of this insidious condition called "depression."

We are dealing with a subject that has all but consumed the attention of our modern culture. It is a condition that has risen to epidemic proportion, having a crippling effect upon our workforce in America. Millions of dollars are lost annually by corporations due to various forms of depression among employees. Unfortunately, the church at large is also inundated with this problem; it is not uncommon to meet believers who take high and frequent doses of anti-depressant medication. Is this a valid remedy for depression?

I'm fully aware that I am traveling a difficult and controversial road in addressing this subject, but it's time to take a hard and honest look at this problem. For too long we have trusted psychology and medical science to solve issues that are clearly addressed in God's book, the Bible. Christian leaders have compromised with the secular and ineffective "treatments" of modern psychiatry, not realizing the true remedy found in the very Word they proclaim.[3]

PROLOGUE

Let me state up front one simple ingredient of "depression;" it is the problem of dwelling on the *past* which causes frustration and failure in the *present*. As one has said, to be 'bemoaning the past and regretting all the things you have not done, you are crippling yourself and preventing yourself from working in the present." We might ask, "is that the way the Christian faith should operate?" The answer is obviously, "No!" Hopefully, the remedy to this dilemma will unfold in the course of reading this book.

Certainly there are complex mental disorders that may incorporate the assistance of mental health professionals. I am not speaking now about extreme cases of clinical depression, where patients spend most of their time in a daze and/or in a fetal position. I'm not sure how many of those on that level can be rescued. Therefore, we must focus on the myriads of people who have not gotten to that extreme condition, but are in the early stages of depression.

PART I

SETTING THE STAGE

Chapter One

How Did We Get Here?

My underlying confidence in dealing squarely with this subject comes from the conviction that God's Word has the ultimate answer to this dilemma. Evolutionary science and medicine have no clue as to man's origin and God-given function. If man began as "a piece of **goo**, ending up in the **zoo**, and now it's **you**," then who are we really? If I am the descendant of a turkey or a fruit fly, then what is my purpose in being here and where am I going? Science has no valid explanation for those vital questions. But in Genesis 2:7, it says:

> *"And the LORD God formed man of the dust of the ground, and breathed into his nostrils the breath of life; and man became a living soul."*

Man: His God-given Purpose and Function

The Lord made man directly out of clay and placed something in him that was not only world-conscious, but God-conscious—namely, a spirit (soul). This inner function made him more than a body, or hunk of protoplasm with arms and legs. This "breath of life" (Heb. *Neshamah*) produced a real person within who became accountable to his Creator. Now there was more to deal with other than mere human flesh. Into man's spirit was placed a conscience, the voice or witness of God within. Man was now responsible for his actions.

So God made or manufactured man for His glory and purpose. Like any responsible manufacturer, He gave him a manual to go with the product. In this case, it is called the Bible. It states how and why he was made, what happened when Adam sinned, and what provision has been made to remedy his fallen condition. Wow! This manual addresses all the basic principles of human life on this planet. We could say in acrostic form that the BIBLE grants us **B**asic **I**nstruction **B**efore **L**eaving **E**arth!

Why Drugs?

As a counselor, I constantly witness the effects of both legal and illegal drugs. In most cases the results are very similar. Every so often someone poses the question: "Why do so many people take drugs?" I can only cite that humans are needy souls, looking for something to relieve the pains of daily existence. This is a tough world. We came in upside down (head first) and we leave with a struggle; the journey between the womb and tomb is a rough one, at best. For many, it is unbearable.

What is a person to do with his troubles? What about the guilt of sin and the violation of his conscience, not to mention the physical and mental stresses that plague a human soul living in a world riddled with hatred and loneliness? In light of what people face every day between home and work, I marvel that the number of those depressed is not higher. I know that apart from God's mercy, I could easily be one of the statistics. I have personally been in that dark, painful pit of despair and am glad to announce in this writing that there is indeed a way out of the dark. This "demon" can be defeated!

I do not treat this subject lightly nor mean to be simplistic about its condition or cure. However, neither do I want to compromise with those who make depression a mental illness which must be tolerated 'til death'. It is certainly valid to mention that God allows bouts with depression, as with other conditions, to further our spiritual maturity. (1Peter 1:6,7)

CHAPTER 1: HOW DID WE GET HERE?

This principle is certainly illustrated by the Biblical patriarch Job. (See Job 1-2) Under God's direction and permission, Job is exposed to horrendous trials and the attack of Satan. He is accused of serving God for material and financial gain, but God challenges Satan to prove his theory, granting the Devil authority to strip Job's possessions (1:12). When Job passes that test, the enemy is then granted permission to touch Job physically (2:4-6). The saga ends with Job's survival and victory over one of the most severe attacks of Hell ever perpetrated on a child of God.

Therefore, we must be careful to rightly diagnose our situation. The source of our dilemma is important to decipher. Not all physical conditions are simply physical. It takes wisdom and discernment to know whether we are dealing with a sheer medical condition or a spiritual attack. While God certainly allows these trials for His purposes, we must not conclude that there is no way out of the dark. Thus, to insist that a believer must spend years on end living under a black cloud of despair is a contradiction of the abundant power of the Gospel of God's grace.

It was the late D. Martyn Lloyd-Jones, a renowned English preacher, who said:

> "Unhappy Christians are, to say the least, a poor recommendation for the Christian Faith. And there can be little doubt but that exuberant joy in the early Christians was one of the most potent factors in the spread of Christianity."[4]

The great Spurgeon said: "The most powerful of all sermons is joyful holiness." By "joyful" he was not suggesting mere laughter or frivolity, but that fullness of the Spirit which fills the believer's soul with heavenly rapture. Holiness, likewise, is not to be confused with "long-faced" morbidity. God has called us to be sanctified, or set apart, for His purposes. In Him we are made whole, or sound, thus reflecting the Spirit's holiness through our lives.

In fact, our bodies have become the temple of the Holy Spirit whereby we have the privilege of glorifying God (1Corinthians 6:19-20). This is another way of saying that we live our lives in such a way that God's character is displayed, and Christ looks great! That is, when people observe how we spend our money, care for family, house, business, church, etc., they know that we are not absorbed in this world but live with eternity in view. How powerful it is to witness a believer who demonstrates this divine combination of godliness (literally, God-likeness) and exuberant joyfulness![5]

Chapter Two

The Early Stage of Depression

Depression begins somewhere. It is not an airborne virus or disease which attacks the body, nor is it primarily a mental disorder, as many claim. However, it does find root in one's thinking process; indeed, it is an attack upon the mind. This is illustrated in the following:

> "It was once announced that the devil was going out of business and would offer all his tools for sale to whoever would pay his price. On the night of the sale they were all very attractively displayed, and a bad-looking lot they were. Malice, hatred, envy, jealousy, sensuality, deceit, and all the other implements of evil were spread out, each marked with its price. Apart from the rest lay a harmless looking wedge-shaped tool, much worn and priced higher than any of them.
>
> Someone asked the devil what it was.
>
> 'That's discouragement,' was his reply.
>
> 'Well, why do you have it priced so high?'
>
> 'Because,' replied the devil, 'it is more useful to me than any of the others. I can pry open and get inside a man's consciousness with that when I could not get near him with any of the others; and when once inside I can use him in whatever way suits me best. It is so much worn because I use it with nearly everybody, as

very few people yet know it belongs to me.'

It hardly needs to be added that the devil's price for discouragement was so high that it was never sold. He still owns it and is still using it."

----Selected

Self-centeredness: Nothing New

This is not to say that Satan arbitrarily runs slip shod over people, but he does engage their reasoning ability. This is clear from his strategy toward the first couple in the Garden of Eden. His initial approach to Eve was in the form of a question: *"Yea, hath God said, Ye shall not eat of every tree of the garden?"* (Genesis 3:1) This is vitally significant, because it subtly challenges what God said—namely, His Word! That becomes the whole basis of the temptation, sin, and eventual fall of humanity.

But there is another factor here that is often overlooked. Satan was not only challenging God's word (command), but also the goodness of God's character. Here was a subtle slander of God's graciousness pertaining to the full provision of their needs. Why would God withhold anything from them? Was He hiding something that really should be theirs? Well, that's just not fair!

How clever and snaky was this classic temptation of the Serpent! Notice that the tempter never commended God for anything. He said nothing about the beauty and bountiful provision of this paradise on earth. Rather, he fostered discouragement and discontentment in Eve's heart by questioning the Lord's loving-kindness and goodness in their behalf.

CHAPTER 2: THE EARLY STAGE OF DEPRESSION

Isn't that the way it works with us as well? We have so much in our part of the world, and yet we never seem satisfied. It is so easy to emphasize what we don't have, rather than to be grateful for what is ours. We are blessed beyond measure and yet so prone to complain. The all too popular mentality is to ask: "What is in it for me?" We are possessed by self, which is the essence of sin. Thus, whatever comes our way is never sufficient. This greedy spirit further produces discontentment, which in turn makes life discouraging.

It is important to note that self-centeredness is an inner mental attitude. When the apostle John speaks of *"the lust of the eyes, the lust of the flesh, and the pride of life"* (1John 2:15), he is referring to the sinful nature (mind) of man. Solomon put it another way: *"As a man thinketh in his heart, so is he."* (Proverbs 23:7) Worldly pleasure and power are attractive because of the gravitation of our fleshly nature. Remember that even Lucifer himself fell from his heavenly estate, not by getting drunk, but by his prideful lust for power!

We could also mention here the "hurt" of being rejected by others, the disappointment in losing a job or advancement, grief over health and family issues, a divorce or the death of a loved one, etc. These can be traumatic challenges which need to be handled properly by God's grace.

Beware of the so-called "prosperity gospel" in the church, which is patterned after the "self-esteem" message of modern psychology. This humanistic philosophy bypasses man's fallen nature and the need to be born again by God's grace through Christ. Man has always attempted to save himself and build self-esteem; his cry has been: "I did it my way." This same mentality has invaded the church in the form of "doing our thing with Jesus' help." What havoc this has produced, leaving in its path a multitude of depressed and disillusioned saints!

Little Things Unchecked Become Big

In a day when so much emphasis is placed on violence, drugs and sex, it is uncanny how many people are ensnared by the insidious power of discouragement. True Christians are very much aware of the "big" sins like adultery, drunkenness, murder, robbery, and the like. I would say that relatively few believers are engaged in such activities. Certainly, we have taken a stand against the gross sins of the flesh, and now, as new creatures in Christ, we live moral lives. Drugs and alcohol, for instance, are no longer part of our lifestyle—we have victory over our old ways. Yet, is it not ironic, how lethal are the remaining "little" sins of our flesh, like worry, fear, self-pity, and resentment!

We are not lacking in this day for psychological explanations for depression, which some refer to as "burnout." Genetic predisposition is cited for its cause; that is, my parents were depressed, thus I have this "disease" in my genes. Others would blame their "mid-life crisis," whether male or female. Still others use their temperament, personality, and nationality as causes. Lastly, many say they are overworked and cannot cope with the pressures of life. While there may be some validity in the above responses, they cannot rightly explain nor justify the epidemic proportion of this problem. Again we are faced with accepting the theories and hypotheses of human psychology as opposed to God's infallible Textbook of Life, called the Bible. It is the purpose of this book to clearly demonstrate the life-changing remedies from the Manual of Life given to man by his Manufacturer.

Discouragement is commonly defined as the condition where someone is "deprived of courage, hope or confidence—to be disheartened." Like other inward conditions, it can be hidden and go undetected, but eventually takes its toll. Fear and resentment may begin to mount, bringing further devastation to

CHAPTER 2: THE EARLY STAGE OF DEPRESSION

our inner being. It has been rightly observed that what "eats us" will do more damage in the long run than just what we eat!

This principle is addressed in Song of Solomon 2:15, when the king says, *"Take us the foxes, the little foxes, that spoil the vines: for our vines have tender grapes."* This has reference to the love relationship between the Bridegroom (Christ) and his bride (the Church). It also illustrates the intimacy of love between a husband and wife which is sensitive and sacred and must be guarded from even the smallest element of confusion or division. How much more is this true in our spiritual fellowship with Christ!

So this is likened to the "little foxes" that cannot adequately reach the grapes, but gnaw at the tender roots of the vine. They kill, as it were, the full productivity of the harvest by operating underground. How insidious are these invaders who, like termites, destroy from within! Does this not speak to the human spirit which is vital and must be protected at any cost? Satan is fully aware of the importance of heart maintenance; he knows the truth of Proverbs 4:23, which states: *"Keep thy heart with all diligence; for out of it are the issues of life."* We need to know it too.

We have several new Rhododendrons planted in the front of our house. I've noticed several fresh mole tunnels around the plant base. I wondered why the leaves were drooping so badly, in spite of constant watering. Apparently there was an attack on the root system by creatures who could not reach the leaves. My effort to water the plants was futile without first dealing with the invaders. So it is that we must confront our "root problems" if we are to bear the right kind of fruit!

Unchecked discouragement quickly leads to depression, which literally means to be "pressed down." Many believers these days are just that: "Pressed down" or under a load, and they can't get up! They have been discouraged for a prolonged period of time which has led to a depressed state. When not addressed properly, i.e., Biblically, many end up on prescription drugs, which at best only relieve symptoms. In the midst of confusion and misinformation, it is time to consider the causes of depression. Likewise, it must be reiterated again that there is indeed a cure for this horrendous condition apart from mind-altering drugs!

It Happens to the Best

David the Psalmist gives us an honest appraisal of his defeated spirit in Psalm 42. He begins with the well-known phrase: *"As the hart (deer) panteth after the water brooks, so panteth my soul after thee, O God. My soul thirsteth for God, for the living God: when shall I come and appear before God?"* Many believers have tried to emulate these words, being misled by David's seemingly "sold out" heart for God, but a closer examination of this passage will reveal a disheartened man, being oppressed by his ungodly peers.

Here is a man who wants the LORD to come and literally rescue him from the present dilemma. His desire is to escape those who constantly taunt him with, *"Where is thy God?"* (Psalm 42:3) His enemies are relentless in demanding living proof of his faith. David gets tired of it and cries not only for deliverance from trial, but from the world! So it is today with many who want to see God for the wrong reasons. We too may be looking for an easy escape hatch to circumvent tribulation, but God has called us to "occupy" (labor) until He comes, while we hide in the Rock of Ages.

This is so uncharacteristic of David when we consider, for example, his extraordinary courage against Goliath. This present trial had to be minuscule compared to his battle with the giant. Yet, this illustrates how insidious and powerful is the spirit of fear that culminates in depression. It seems to "grab"

CHAPTER 2: THE EARLY STAGE OF DEPRESSION

its victim, creating a desire to flee *"when no man pursueth."* In some respect, the mental "giants" are more difficult to confront than the physical, but that only heightens the necessity for them to be conquered. The demonic attack here is more insidious than that of Goliath himself. It is imperative, therefore, to examine David's strategy against his bout with depression.

Notice how he addresses the issue head on when he exclaims, *"Why art thou cast down, O my soul? and why art thou disquieted* (literally, 'shook up') *in me? hope thou in God: for I shall yet praise him..."* (Psalm 42:5) Rather than *listening* to himself (i.e., feeding on defeated thoughts), he *talks* to himself on the basis of truth. This is faith in action—rebuking ourselves from God's Word and deliberately choosing to hope in the Sovereign God! Hence we have here a choice preview of turning discouragement into encouragement and triumph.

Supernatural Provision

The child of God is not to be *"drunk with wine,"* but certainly he is to be filled or intoxicated by the Holy Spirit (Ephesians 5:18). The spirit of this age has mesmerized and bewitched the church at large, intoxicating us with the wrong substance. Indeed, we have been robbed of the "wine" (Spirit) of heaven who delights to control and direct the believer into the fullness of God's blessing. Isaiah exclaims and Jesus adds:

> *"Ho, every one that thirsteth, come ye to the waters, and he that hath no money; come ye, buy and eat; yea, come buy wine and milk without money and without price." (Isaiah 55:1)*

> *"Blessed are they which do hunger and thirst after righteousness, for they shall be filled." (Matthew 5:6)*

What are we seeking? What captures our interest? We are what we think, nothing more! We cannot live in a vacuum, for we must be filled with or controlled by something. So Paul says:

> *"Let the word of Christ dwell in you richly in all wisdom...singing with grace in your hearts to the Lord." (Colossians 3:16)*

Notice that the Word and the Spirit work together to fill us to overflowing so we can cope with all the challenges of life.

Let us proceed to the heart of the matter by considering the causes of depression. We will approach the subject first from causes that are surface or symptomatic. Finally we will examine the root or foundational causes. May God give us insight, direction, and overcoming grace to explore this momentous subject.

PART II

SURFACE CAUSES OF DEPRESSION

Chapter Three

Unfulfilled Goals

It is necessary to explore just why and how depression occurs. Is it just a physical disease, like the flu? Is it something found in a person's genes or DNA? Does it come as a result of childhood abuse? What about disappointments in life? Is it rooted deeply within the psyche or soul? No doubt, many more reasons have been offered to explain this complex condition. Somehow we need to sort out these "causes" as to how directly or indirectly they trigger depression.

For example, if I were discussing the causes of divorce, what reasons would I give? One of the most common causes mentioned is finances, or money problems. Is that the primary cause of a couple's separation, or is it a result of other factors in the relationship? You can say, "They split over money," but what else has been going on in their lives? Thus it would be vital for a counselor to explore the various factors culminating in their divorce. If they have been resentful and spiteful toward each other, for instance, then would money constitute the primary concern? It would seem obvious that their heart relationship would have to be addressed and healed before there could be any permanent financial remedy. This same principle is applicable to our discussion of depression.

The following "causes" mentioned in this chapter are perceived by this writer as being surface or peripheral in essence. Other counselors and mental professionals may "lump" these factors together, with no relevant distinction, but the acid test is what must be addressed to bring a decided cure for depression. My thesis here is that although the following surface causes may be overcome, the root problems which actually trigger depression will still be present. With that understanding, let us consider the following:

One of the common causes of discouragement and subsequent depression is *unfulfilled goals*. Any ambitious soul on earth has had dreams of the future. We've all projected in our minds what and where we would like to be at a given time or stage. Some have thought seriously about early retirement with plenty of money in the bank. Others have counted on being at least vice-president of their corporation by age 45 with a BMW car in the garage. Others labor for the day when they can buy a summer home on the lake with a yacht to match. What happens if and when these goals do not materialize?

I've observed that parents often project themselves into their children. Aspirations and plans yet unfulfilled in their lives are thrust upon the kids, hoping that the fulfillment will be realized in their offspring. The father, for instance, who always wanted to be a football star, now pressures his young son to pursue that sport despite the boy having little interest or ability. Likewise, the mother who excelled as a pianist is now discouraged because her daughter has no interest in playing the piano.

These are real examples of how disappointment in ourselves and others can frustrate our plans. The same principle holds true in the work of the ministry. Pastors and church leaders often set dated goals for Sunday school attendance, number of new converts, etc., only to be disheartened when it falls short. Certainly no one can fault a diligent pastor for anticipating the rich blessing of God upon his labors. However, the success of his ministry is not primarily focused on how many he has in the church, but how faithful he has been to His Lord!

The apostle Paul speaks to this issue when he says:

"Moreover it is required in stewards that a man be found faithful...Therefore judge nothing before the time, until the Lord

CHAPTER 3: UNFULFILLED GOALS

come, who both will bring to light the hidden things of darkness; and will make manifest the counsels of the hearts; and then shall every man have praise of God." (1Corinthians 4:2,5)

We may be counting heads while God is weighing hearts. It may not be the case of how *many* in the congregation, but rather how *much*. Thus, we must *"preach the word; be instant in season, out of season; reprove, rebuke, exhort with all longsuffering and doctrine."* (2 Timothy 4:2) After all, only God can give life to the seed and produce a harvest.

Paul further levels the playing field by stating how God uses all kinds of ministers to build His kingdom:

"I have planted, Apollos watered; but God gave the increase. So then neither is he that planteth any thing, neither he that watereth; but God that giveth the increase. Now he that planteth and he that watereth are one; and every man shall receive his own reward according to his labor. For we are labourers together with God..." (1Corinthians 3:6-9a)

Thus it behooves ministers of the Word to be faithful in God's vineyard, effectively using their gifts to glorify the Lord. Forget about how God is working through other personalities, for we are all on the same team. Thank Him for the privilege of laboring with the Holy Spirit in our particular niche. The results are in His hands. Let us therefore be *"...stedfast, unmovable, always abounding in the work of the Lord, forasmuch as ye know that your (*our*) labor is not in vain in the Lord."* (1Corinthians 15:58) This certainly is an antidote to ministerial depression and eventual burnout.

Elijah's Disappointment

It would be well for us to explore some Biblical examples of our subject. The prophet Elijah surely gives us insight as to how disappointment and depression can profoundly grip the soul of God's servants. In I Kings 18-19, we have the moving narrative of Elijah's confrontation with King Ahab and his 430 prophets of Baal. God's people Israel were backslidden, "sitting on the fence" regarding the supremacy of Jehovah over Baal. Elijah challenges them to decide whether they will serve Jehovah or Baal as the true and living God.

He proposes a showdown with the Baal worshippers to determine who is indeed LORD of all. They are to lay the sacrifice on the altar but light no fire under it. Elijah would do the same, only he dug wide trenches around the altar and completely drenched the sacrifice with water. Then he uttered the challenge that both parties would call on their deity, and whoever answered by fire, consuming the sacrifice, would be declared LORD and GOD. Thus Elijah would expose and ridicule their apostate religion. He would demonstrate the miraculous display of Jehovah's power, watching fire descend from Heaven and consuming the water-soaked sacrifice.

The false prophets had labored all day appeasing their gods, but there was no fire. Elijah's time came to answer the challenge and after a brief prayer—the fire fell! Pandemonium broke out as the True God revealed Himself anew; the Israelites fell on their faces proclaiming: "The LORD, He is (the) God," while the prophets of Baal were slain by Elijah.

What a victory was won that day! How heroic and bold was this prophet. Wouldn't such an event bring widespread notoriety to Elijah? Why, he could bask in that experience for years to come. But such was not the case. Amazingly, we find

CHAPTER 3: UNFULFILLED GOALS

him literally running for his life after receiving a "telegram" from Queen Jezebel who threatened to kill him (1Kings 19:2-3)![6]

Furthermore, we see him under a tree in the wilderness, pleading with God to take his life. This desire to die was certainly more than just a panic attack. How is it that this great prophet could have such a victorious mountain-top experience one day and become an emotional cripple the next? Did he catch "mental depression" while jogging over the landscape? How does it happen?

Let me suggest that what happened to Elijah is essentially what happens to all of God's people who seriously walk by faith. God answered Elijah's prayer and granted him a euphoric victory on the mount. He walked in God's authority and blessing as long as he focused on Jehovah's person and character. But that was shattered through an accusatory message sent by the hand of a demon-possessed woman. He feared only God up to this point, but now his eye of faith changed focus, and unbelief welcomed the spirit of fear. I'm referring to a satanic attack upon this courageous preacher of righteousness. What else could have produced such cowardice?

Young Timothy, of New Testament fame, was faced with similar bouts of fear. It appears that he was sensitive by nature and easily intimidated. Paul exhorts him to "stir up the gift" of the Spirit's power within, because:

> *"God hath not given us the spirit of fear; but of power, and of love, and of a sound mind. Be not thou therefore ashamed of the testimony of our Lord...but be thou partaker of the afflictions of the gospel according to the power of God." (2 Timothy 1:7,8)*

You see, when we fear God, we need not fear anyone else. But Satan is the "accuser of the brethren" (Revelation 12:10) who delights in slandering our motives and attacking our faith. I suspect that Elijah was disappointed that Ahab and Jezebel were not among the Hebrew converts when the fire fell. He expected a "clean sweep" with no opposition—but such was not the case. His goal was lofty, but it didn't work out as anticipated.

His issue was not only with Jezebel, but with God Himself, that is, the Lord didn't do exactly what Elijah expected. Is that not a common problem among the saints of God? The pastor preaches and two people respond to the invitation. Rejoicing follows for a time until the pastor hears a whisper in his ear, "How come six didn't come forward"? Immediately, the joy is replaced by a questioning spirit. How easily we are dissuaded from a position of victory to one of defeat! Rather than submissively walking with God and obeying His will, we are set up for a fall by second-guessing what we think God should do in the circumstance.

Chapter Four

Losing Sight of God

Failure to see our goals and expectations materialize can bring great disappointment and frustration. However, another cause of discouragement of soul is the subtlety of losing sight of God. How easy it becomes to get caught up with our work and ministry for God and lose the sense of God's presence. I say it's subtle because it can happen so easily when we are caught up in what we are doing for God. Yes, it is possible to be so involved in the work of the Lord that we fail to see the Lord of the work! That failure eventually spells defeat.

The Exodus from the Ministry

Quite some time ago, I received a religious news story over the Internet called: "Hundreds of Pastors Leave Their Ministry Each Month" by Eric Tiansay.[7] In this article he cites various findings by groups who study this clergy phenomenon.

According to the Alban Institute in Washington, D.C., at least 17 percent of clergy suffer from stress or burnout. It goes on to say that some 1400 ministers a year call a toll-free hot line of the Southern Baptist Convention which counsels ministers through its LeaderCare program. It's estimated that nearly 100 of its pastors leave their ministry each month.

SunScape Ministries of Colorado, which serves clergy in crises, reported that in all denominations nationwide 1,600 ministers a month are terminated or forced to resign their pulpit. That is 19,000 each year – not including missionaries in foreign cultures. That figure is nothing less than staggering! Consider the following reasons given by pastors that contribute to their depression and failure:

- 94% of pastors say they feel pressure to have a perfect family.
- 90% feel inadequately trained to cope with ministry demands.
- 80% say that ministry has a negative impact on their own families.
- 70% say their self-esteem was higher before entering ministry.
- 40% consider quitting every Monday morning.
- 25% of clergy marriages end in divorce.[8]

This study indicates an unprecedented epidemic among church leaders in America! If this is the state of under-shepherds, then what must be the condition of the sheep who follow? The ancient Chaucer once said, "If gold rusts, what will iron do"? The issue of godly leadership and example must be addressed from a Biblical perspective, and not relegated to some "mental illness" or psychological condition.

After all, whose work is it anyway? From those in leadership to the lowliest saint, the principle is the same: *"Faithful is he that calleth you, who also will do it."* (1 Thessalonians 5:24) That is, the One who calls us to do His bidding also gives the impetus and power to do it. Paul also encourages our confidence in God when he says, *"...he* (the Lord) *which hath begun a good work in you will perform it until the day of Jesus Christ."* (Philippians 1:6) In other words, what God starts He continues and consummates! That godly work begun in us will never fail but will be brought to completion by the God who started it. Amen!

Well then, what is our responsibility in this process? How do we cooperate with this ongoing work of grace? The apostle seems to address the whole scenario when he commands the saints, in Philippians 2:12-13, to *"work out your own salvation with fear and trembling"* (proper attitude of

CHAPTER 4: LOSING SIGHT OF GOD

gratefulness and humility), *"for* (because) *it is God which worketh in you both to will and to do of his good pleasure"* (will or plan). What a beautiful exhortation is this! How is it to be understood?

Notice he does not say: Work **up** your salvation—that's impossible, for only Jesus Christ Himself on the Cross did all the work necessary to save sinners. Rather, we work **out** what God is working **in**! Salvation is of the Lord, and by His Spirit He is producing His life and purpose in and through His servant saints. Yes, the very character of Jesus Christ is potentially operating in each of His children—called *"the fruit of the Spirit,* (which) *is "love, joy, peace, longsuffering, gentleness, goodness, faith, meekness, temperance"* (Galatians 5:22-23). It is in this context that our work and ministry must be executed. God is working out His secret will (unknown to us) while we obey His revealed will (the Word of God). Let us do what we know to be right while God continues to exercise His Sovereign plan in the background. This concept is further captured in Romans 8:28-29:

> *"And we know that all things work together for good to them that love God, to them who are the called according to his purpose. For whom he did foreknow, he also did predestinate to be conformed to the image of his Son, that he might be the firstborn among many brethren."*

It is essential to realize that if we are believers, we were saved on purpose for a purpose. Therefore, the "all things" in every situation are working together toward that purpose—namely, that we should be "conformed" (literally, jointly formed or similar) to Christ's image. God has planned ahead of time ("predestined") that we shall look like Jesus. To know that glorious truth will enable us to respond properly, rather than react improperly, in the midst of difficult circumstances.

The verse does **not** say that "all things are good." This could be misconstrued by some to teach fatalism—namely, that there is no God, nor plan, but all is left to chance. Thus, "whatever happens, happens." No! Our God has an eternal purpose regarding those "who love God"—that's a believer, not just anyone. The saint can be assured that all things, events, and even people, somehow blend together for God's glory and our good. There is tremendous liberation in this truth.

A common illustration is in order. With fondness I visualize the endless number and assortment of homemade cakes produced over the years by my wife. Yet, thinking about the process is not very appetizing. Ingredients like flour, sugar, salt, eggs, vanilla, shortening, etc., were all placed separately into the mixing bowl. What a conglomeration! To eat a tablespoon full of that "gunk" would sicken the stomach for sure. Yet when mixed properly, placed in the cake pan and baked in the oven at the right time and temperature, something magical happens. The finished product, especially with the whipped-cream topping, is absolutely delicious!

How great is our God, to take the "ingredients" of our lives and eventually bring forth a finished product that will bring glory to Him and blessing to us! I like to define God's grace as His bringing fruit out of a garbage pail. He's a God of miracles and wants to demonstrate that grace in your life, my friend. Maybe you have never really met this God through Jesus Christ and have come to realize that He alone is the Savior from sin. He came to die for sinners that they might be rescued from sin's power and penalty, and yes, He wants to give you new and abundant life with freedom to love and serve Christ. He calls on you to repent (turn to Him from sin) and believe (trust) Him to save you today.

CHAPTER 4: LOSING SIGHT OF GOD

> *"For God so loved the world, that He gave His only begotten Son, that whosoever believeth in him should not perish, but have everlasting life. For God sent not his Son into the world to condemn the world; but that the world through him might be saved." (John 3:16-17)*

What a wonderful work He did in my life over 50 years ago when I cried out to Him for salvation! It was like a 300-pound bag of cement had been lifted from my shoulders. And while the trials and difficulties have been many, He has granted abundant strength to persevere. For the God who saves us also keeps us along life's journey. The One who took our sins on the Cross also carries our burdens. He bids us to "cast all of our care (anxiety) upon Him, because He cares for us." (1Peter 5:7) Jesus says further:

> *"Come unto me, all ye that labor and are heavy laden, and I will give you rest. Take my yoke upon you, and learn of me; for I am meek and lowly in heart; and ye shall find rest unto your souls. For my yoke is easy, and my burden is light." (Matthew 11:28-30)*

My friend, there **is** a glorious rest in Christ in the midst of this turbulent world. Stop here and consider your plight, for you need not continue with a heavy, depressed heart. Christ will lift that burden when you throw it on Him and replace it with His peace. Trust Him NOW! This challenge to you may be the most important part of this book. Don't treat it lightly.

Moses' Disillusionment

The problem of frustration and burnout is nothing new. Take the confrontation between God and Moses regarding the rebellious people under his charge (Numbers 11:10-17). Following the miraculous Red Sea opening, it was then just a matter of time before they reached the Promised Land. However, there was much that Moses didn't anticipate, as depicted in this passage of Scripture.

Wouldn't it have been encouraging if the people had simply obeyed the Lord and His servant Moses? Instead, they became discontented with God's dietary provision (i.e., manna) and began complaining, while demanding flesh to eat. The Lord responded in displeasure and judgment (Numbers11:1), while Moses successfully pled their case in prayer. God's servant saved the day and certainly now the people would respond obediently. Not so! Instead, they began to lust and weep all the more, desiring to return to Egypt. Moses took this whole thing personally and thus addressed the Lord (Numbers 11:11f):

> *"Wherefore* (why) *hast thou afflicted thy servant? and wherefore have I not found favour in thy sight, that thou layest the burden of all this people upon me? Have I conceived all this people? ...Whence* (where) *should I have flesh to give all this people?...I am not able to bear all this people alone, because it is too heavy for me. And if thou deal thus with me, kill me..."*

Has there ever been a sincere, committed Christian leader who could not identify with Moses' dilemma? Remember the early days? How new and fresh it was to begin in ministry with an enthusiastic heart to please God! What a privilege to be able and enabled to proclaim His eternal, all-powerful Word. How eager the people were to hear and follow your pastoral discourses—it was like heaven on earth. In fact, you even received a "pay check" for doing what you yourself would pay to do.

CHAPTER 4: LOSING SIGHT OF GOD

Then came the ripples in the stream, when some of the enthusiasm began to subside. The unusual became quite usual, and the response of others was not what it was before. Some people became critical and discontented—yes, even those who at first seemed so close and friendly. Family pressures began to mount, and soon you started second-guessing your call. The Word didn't seem to refresh your soul as it once did, and even God seemed quite distant in prayer. You became discouraged and even resentful toward the people whom you had come to serve. And when it didn't get better, you began to lash out at God Himself, as did Moses. Sound familiar?

Thankfully, God was fully aware of Moses' dilemma, and had a remedy for his situation. In Numbers 11:16f, the Lord exhorts him to gather from among the people 70 elders (leaders) to share the burden of the ministry. This idea was planted in Moses several years before when Jethro, his father-in-law, exhorted him to delegate responsibility to others (Exodus 18:17ff). It was clear to Jethro that Moses would soon be "burned out" if he didn't receive help in counseling the multitudes. The prophet was quick to follow that wise advice.

Now, in the midst of further crises, Moses obeys God and selects the 70 elders. This multiplication of leadership proved to be an asset to all concerned. *"And the Lord came down...and took of the spirit that was upon him* (Moses) *and gave it unto the seventy elders"* (Numbers 11:25). There was enough of the Spirit of God for all concerned. Moses' ministry was now greatly enhanced and enlarged through others who were anointed by the same Spirit. What a cure for burnout!

Whatever your dilemma may be, God has a tailor-made answer for your situation. The psalmist said, *"Thy word is a lamp unto my feet and a light unto my path."* (Psalm 119:105) Indeed, as we seek to obey His word and cry out for wisdom (James 1:5), we too, as with Moses of old, will find direction and remedy. After all, He said, *"I will never* (literally, 'no never') *leave thee nor forsake thee* (no never)." (Hebrews 13:5)!

Jeremiah's Mood Swings

There's hardly a more graphic example in Scripture of a "manic-depressive" than the prophet Jeremiah. If anyone could be psychologically labeled as having mental problems, it was he. His candor in describing his condition and circumstance is almost brutal. Yet, he ultimately finds his deliverance and remedy in the faithfulness of God and His Word.

Just an overview of Jeremiah 20 reveals the prophet's "yo-yo" experience or, as some might call it, an emotional "roller-coaster ride." Note his mood swings: He's **up** (vs. 1-6); he's **down** (vs. 7-9); he's **up** (vs. 10-13); he's **down** (vs. 14-18)! All this is happening in the backdrop of God's divine call to Jeremiah:

> *"Before I formed in the belly I knew thee; and before thou camest forth out of the womb I sanctified thee; and I ordained thee a prophet unto the nations. Then said I, Ah, Lord God; behold, I cannot speak, for I am a child. But the LORD said unto me, Say not, thou art a child: for thou shalt go to all that I shall send thee, and whatsoever I command thee thou shalt speak. Be not afraid of their faces, for I am with thee to deliver thee...Behold, I have put my words in thy mouth. See, I have this day set thee over the nations...to root out, and to pull down, and to destroy, and to throw down, to build and to plant." (Jeremiah 1:5-10)*

What an all-inclusive and comprehensive call is this

CHAPTER 4: LOSING SIGHT OF GOD

from the Almighty! Set apart as a prophet of God from his mother's womb, he is given specific directions and equipping right from the start. Included in this commission is direction as to his location, the people involved, the message to preach, and the promise of boldness and God's protection. Wow! What preacher wouldn't relish such a backing, and yet in time even Jeremiah lost sight of that miraculous call.

May I address the pastors who are reading these words. Preacher, God has given you the same promise of His omnipotent support and leading. Believe it, and don't lose its focus! If you **do** lose it, then repent and refocus! I believe the Lord has incorporated Jeremiah's example into His Word to exhibit what can happen to any of God's servants who begin to walk by sight and feeling, rather than by faith.

Let's consider briefly how low the depressed prophet got. Jeremiah was going "great guns" in his faithful denunciation of the sins of Judah until chapter 20 where we find him preaching at the temple site. He seemed to have a more favorable response on the street than at the "church house." In fact, his rebuking message stirs the anger of Pashur, the priest, who strikes Jeremiah and throws him in jail (vs. 1,2).
During this difficult time, the prophet makes some astounding statements, possibly over-shadowed only by the Lord Jesus Himself, when He cried, *"My God, my God, why hast thou forsaken me?"* In verse 7, Jeremiah vents his issue with God by saying, *"O LORD, thou hast deceived me, and I was deceived: thou art stronger than I...I am in derision daily, every one mocketh me."*

What is this man saying? Who, in all of Scripture, has ever accused God Almighty of such a thing—deception on God's part? What was going through the prophet's mind? Was this not just an honest confrontation between a disillusioned servant of God and his Director? Maybe so, but it's clear that

Jeremiah has lost sight of his commission from the Lord, thus opening the door for confusion and depression.

Jeremiah vocalizes what many of us have essentially thought, but would never want anyone else to discover, i.e., the questioning of God's original call. What he anticipated somehow was not lining up with his present experience. Where was the promise of God's presence? "Lord, where are you in this time of suffering? I thought you'd go before me. Why am I having such a tough time? Did I do something wrong? Man, if I knew the ministry was going to be like this, I'm not sure I would have answered the call. You didn't tell me the whole story—you deceived me!"

Sound familiar? This is not far-fetched to someone who is sold out to Christ and finds himself under severe enemy attack. There is one who will take advantage of our lapses of faith—one who *"as a roaring lion, walketh about, seeking whom he may devour."* (I Peter 5:8). Yes, Satan delights in "accusing the brethren before our God day and night" (Revelation 12:10). Job's character and veracity, you remember, were "accused before God." The Devil insisted that Job served the Lord for what he could get out of it, and thus would deny God if those benefits were removed. Adam and Eve, however, were approached by Satan who slandered God's character before the first couple. (Genesis 3) God was made to appear as a tyrant who withheld His goodness by forbidding their partaking of the tree.

This same accusation seems to affect the prophet too. Jeremiah's ministry of the Word has become a "reproach and a daily derision." (Jeremiah 20:8,9) Obviously disillusioned, he decides to keep his mouth shut, not mentioning the Lord nor speaking "any more in His name." How many of the Lord's servants have been here, determined to quit God and the ministry! How increasingly obvious is the connection of the

CHAPTER 4: LOSING SIGHT OF GOD

"demon" spirit with depression!

However, almost in the same breath, the prophet expresses the realization of deep conviction:

> *"But his word was in mine heart as a burning fire shut up in my bones, and I was weary with for-bearing, and I could not stay* (literally, 'hold back').*"(20:9)*

How this illustrates the faithfulness and persevering grace of Jeremiah's God! The prophet can move just so far away from the arena of ministry, and then the Spirit of the Lord tracks him down. O, that love that will not let me go! Even when he wants to quit, there's a resurgence of the fire of God in his soul! Truly, Paul's exhortation applies here:

> *"Faithful is he that calleth you, who also will do it" (1Thessalonians 5:24).*

That initial call upon Jeremiah's life was now being challenged by horrendous trial, but the Lord intervenes and revives His servant's heart in the midst of the circumstance. God met the three Hebrew children in the midst of the fiery furnace and brought them through unscathed and smoke-free. (Daniel 3:27) As someone has said: "What God orders, He pays for."

Jeremiah's experience proves that trials and persecution do not *break us* but rather *make us*! Up until now, believers in the United States have suffered precious little for their faith. In other parts of the world however, like Indonesia, the Philippines, China, and Africa, believers are being imprisoned and slaughtered for their testimony. Fanatical Muslims and other cults are determined to stamp out Christianity, and their threat is rapidly nearing our shores. But this must not deter us from proclaiming the glorious Gospel, which is still the *"power of God unto salvation to every one that believeth"* (Romans 1:16). We must "burn-on," rather than burnout!

Jesus never said it would be easy or convenient to serve Him. He came "not to bring peace, but a sword," i.e., to divide those who believe Him from those who don't. By virtue of being born again, we enter a new family—taking on His friends as well as His enemies. We are now hated by those who once loved us, and all because of our relationship with the Lord Jesus Christ (Matthew 10:36).

> *"Yea, and all that will live godly in Christ Jesus shall suffer persecution" (2 Timothy 3:12).*

Jeremiah knew this principle, and we had better get it straight too! Things don't always work out as we anticipate, which in turn can bring about frustration and discouragement. Life is just that way; it might be wise to "hope for the best, while expecting the worst." We need to be spiritually alert, catching ourselves when our minds are drifting toward depression. Let us choose to do the will of God, despite how we may feel. That's what Jeremiah did.

A Horrendous Test

There's no greater test of Jeremiah's courage and overcoming faith than in the Book of Lamentations. Here the City of Jerusalem lies in shambles, destroyed by the invasion of the Babylonian Empire. It is described as "the funeral of a city." The prophet's predictions have come to pass, with God's judgment falling on disobedient Judah. Devastation is everywhere, and if ever there is a time to be depressed, this is it. On top of it all, Jeremiah bemoans his own distress over what God has allowed him to suffer personally:

CHAPTER 4: LOSING SIGHT OF GOD

> *"I am the man that hath seen affliction by the rod of his (God's) wrath. He hath...brought me into darkness...He turneth his hand against me all the day. My flesh and my skin hath he made old; he hath broken my bones...I was a derision to all my people." (Lamentations 3:1-4,14)*

Jeremiah's experience here seems almost prophetic of the curse and agony laid upon the Lord Jesus Himself. Certainly the prophet enters into this dark chamber of affliction presently surrounding Jerusalem, which appears at best to be hopeless. Yet into the darkness shines a light in his soul when he remembers (begins to focus upon) the character of his Lord. In a powerful exclamation of faith, he cries:

> *"It is of the LORD's mercies that we are not consumed, because his compassions fail not. They are new every morning: **great is thy faithfulness**. The LORD is my portion, saith my soul; therefore will I hope in him...The LORD is good unto them that wait for him, to the soul that seeketh him. It is good that a man should both hope and quietly wait for the salvation of the LORD." (Lamentations 3:22-26)*

Talk about a contradictory experience! Read the whole context of Lamentations 3 and see if you've ever heard a more desolate description of anguish and hopelessness. In such a circumstance, what would ever keep God's servant from utter despair and even suicide? At the very least, he was a candidate for "Prozac!" But to the praise of Jehovah, we witness here a demonstration of His unfailing grace, enabling Jeremiah to focus upon the unchanging, faithful character of His God. The prophet cannot concentrate on the situation without despair, but he chooses rather to look up, seeing His Lord, who is bigger than the situation. That's the means to deliverance from any bout with depression.

It is important to note here that Jeremiah's confidence in God's faithfulness was not some blind trust. Throughout his prophecy, he expounds the displeasure of the Lord over Judah's iniquity and waywardness. God is faithful to His own justice in dealing with His rebellious children; but almost in the same breath, the Lord promises the hope of deliverance from bondage at a later time.[9]

Even in the midst of desolation, Jeremiah trusts the heart of God, even though he can't trace His hand in the present circumstance. *"The LORD is my portion, saith my soul; therefore will I hope in him."* (vs. 24) See here how Jeremiah speaks to himself of God's faithfulness, rather than listening to what he hears or sees around him. He's learning that the LORD Himself is his "portion" (literally, "inheritance, possession"), and that's all he needs to know to anchor his hope. David verifies this truth in Psalm 16:5: *"The LORD is the portion of mine inheritance and of my cup: thou maintainest my lot."* To have the Lord Himself is to have it all!

This understanding is essential to the spiritual arsenal of every child of God. The enemy of our soul will repeatedly slander the goodness of the Lord; thus, we must speak to ourselves on the basis of the Word and conquer by faith. Our focus must be on the One who said, *"I will never leave thee, nor forsake thee."*

Chapter Five

Wrong Response to Trials

Someone has said that it's not only our actions but our reactions that spell victory or defeat in any circumstance. How do we handle the unexpected invasions into our well-ordered world? Responding properly to unforeseen trials is a vital component of the Christian walk. What should our reaction be when faced with unexpected difficulties? James certainly has a word in season when he wrote:

> *"My brethren, count it all joy when ye fall into divers temptations; knowing this, that the trying of your faith worketh patience. But let patience have her perfect work, that ye may be perfect and entire, wanting nothing." (1:2-4)*

Temptation or Trial—Which?

First, let us consider the distinction between temptations and trials. Actually, both of these words come from the same root—relating to testing and discipline (training). The common difference has been explained from the perspective of source and purpose. Simplistically, we could say that temptation comes from Satan to see if we'll fall; while trial comes from God to see if we'll stand. Yet, in either case, the believer must prevail by faith so as to facilitate the development of patience and perfection, or maturity.

Thus, God uses all events in our lives to bring us into full maturity. How is it possible to "count it all joy" when we are tried? Does that mean if we get into a car accident, for instance, that we shout "Hallelujah" as we view the dented fender? I think not.

James says: "Count it all joy," which means to "reckon" it so by faith, because we know that God has a higher purpose in mind. This is a heart attitude, not primarily an emotion, which recognizes that "all things are working together for good;" that is, for God's glory and our edification. This attitude of faith will keep us from going ballistic when placed in a trying and unexpected situation.

It must be remembered that we are saved on purpose for a purpose (Romans 8:28,29), and that the Lord is using "all things" to conform us to the image of Christ. Maturity and perfection come with a price, thus, *"tribulation worketh* (produces) *patience; and patience, experience; and experience, hope: And hope maketh not ashamed; because the love of God is shed abroad in our hearts by the Holy Ghost"* (Romans 5:3-5). It is in the midst of trial that I find the reality of God's sustaining grace; it is there that I gain experience of God's great character, thus my heart is flooded with hope, which in turn anchors or stabilizes my soul.

Be assured that God is at work in our lives, and no event is incidental or superfluous. Knowing this fact in our spirit is the key to spiritual sanity and growth. How we respond to trial is all-important in the scope of God's developmental process in our lives. We can either become bitter or better, depending upon our response to the challenges of everyday life.

Trials of the Faithful

The writer of Hebrews has much to say about the trial of faith. The classic Hall of Faith in chapter eleven, enumerates the many Old Testament saints who believed God in difficult circumstances. For instance, *"by faith Noah...moved with fear, prepared an ark to the saving of his house."* (Hebrews 11:7) Likewise, *"by faith Moses, when he was come to years, refused*

CHAPTER 5: WRONG RESPONSE TO TRIALS

to be called the son of Pharaoh's daughter; Choosing rather to suffer affliction with the people of God, than to enjoy the pleasures of sin for a season; Esteeming the reproach of Christ greater riches than the treasures in Egypt." (11:24-26)

The list goes on of those who by faith were able to face horrendous testing and difficulties with the optimism of hope. They all did something that had not been done before—that's the challenge of faith. In fact, some faced extreme persecution and death, being "stoned...sawn asunder...slain with the sword." (11:33-40) What role models of stalwart faith are set before us here!

In light of this great cloud of witnesses who watch from the grandstand of Heaven, we are challenged to *"lay aside every weight, and the sin which doth so easily beset us, and let us run with patience the race that is set before us"* (Hebrews 12:1). There is great incentive for obedience in knowing that our spiritual forefathers may be observing our actions from Heaven. At least, they have exemplified ("witnessed") that there is sufficient grace to live and/or die for Christ! Such knowledge is encouraging in the daily arena of dealing with personal hindrances.

As mentioned above, a "weight" is a potential sin, something hindering us from being more effective. Constant tardiness would be an example of something hurting our testimony, eventually becoming a sin. Then there's that besetting sin, the one that often recurs in times of weakness. We are exhorted here to "lay aside" any hindrances—to take them off like a garment. I am reminded of a track star who enters the race with a skimpy outfit and feather-light shoes. If he showed up in combat fatigues, boots, helmet, etc., he would be laughed off the track. Not only that, but he would be weighted down sufficiently to make running the race a calamity. The idea is to get rid of all the excess baggage in our lives in order to run the race of life effectively and victoriously.

How is that done? By *"looking unto Jesus the author and finisher of our faith."* (Hebrews 12:2) What does that mean? Well, for starters, Jesus is the Source and chief leader of our faith—all that we are and have comes from Him. Not only that, but He is the perfecter and consummator of our faith. He is the beginning and the end, the Alpha and Omega, the first and the last—and everything in between!

In other words, He who has begun a *"good work in you will perform it until the day of Jesus Christ."* (Philippians 1:6) What He begins, he finishes! But we need to *"work out your own salvation with fear and trembling. For it is God which worketh in you both to will and to do of his good pleasure."* (Philippians 2:12-13) That is, we need to work **out** what God is working **in**. Since trials are part of His work out plan, our response to such is all important.

We are given a glimpse of Jesus' reaction to the ultimate trial—the Cross (Hebrews 12:2-4), which further encourages us in handling trial and suffering. How did our Saviour face the Crucifixion? It says: *"who for* (because of) *the joy that was set before him endured the cross, despising the shame, and is set down at the right hand of the throne of God."* The anguish of His atoning death was superseded or overshadowed by the joyous anticipation of His finished work in behalf of sinners. When the work of redemption was finalized at the Cross, Christ would then ascend back to Heaven, where He would dispense to the saints all the benefits resulting from His sacrifice. Somehow that brought comfort to His soul in light of impending death.

How encouraging is this! If the joy of accomplishing Redemption helped to take the "sting" out of his suffering, how much more should we "consider" his awful plight, *"lest ye be*

CHAPTER 5: WRONG RESPONSE TO TRIALS

wearied and faint in your minds." (vs.3) In other words, if Jesus could endure such opposition and the agony of Hell, why can we not endure the trials of life by His grace? After all, we have not been called upon to suffer and bleed for the sins of humanity, as did Christ. (Hebrews 12:4) Thus, He has become the pioneer of our faith, and we "can do all things through Christ" who strengthens us!

Dear friend, it is very important how we respond to trial. Remember, God is dealing with us as His *children* (12:5); *"for whom the Lord loveth he chasteneth* (disciplines, trains),*"* thus using trials to develop our character and effectiveness. But as His children, we have choices to make regarding this training program. We can either "despise" the discipline, "faint" in the midst of it, or "endure" it. Take your pick!

Despising Trials

The writer exhorts: *"My son, despise not the chastening of the Lord..."* The word for "despise" is used only here and has the idea of "treating lightly" or rejecting the discipline. We can easily detest or loathe the trials of life, developing inner resentment toward God. This is the wrong reaction to difficulty, because it takes lightly the ongoing purpose of the Lord who loves us. Such an attitude indicates unbelief, which is really a slander against the character of our God. We have little understanding of the devastating consequences of our unfaithful actions.

Is it not ironic how believers take up with the world in their response to trials? If things go well, we have a tendency to pat ourselves on the back. If things go wrong, we blame God! This illustrates how we despise the chastening of the Lord, and many times the result is a bitter spirit. Trials can make us bitter or better, depending on how we respond. Most believers I have met and/or counseled are resentful and bitter about something. Just like Cain of old, we get the "it ain't fair" mentality toward God; and to make it worse, we deny that we have an issue with the Lord.

I cannot overemphasize how crucial it is to face resentment toward God. To fail here is to forfeit the key remedy for depression. Note how Cain, of old, was mad at God for not accepting the offering of his labor (Genesis 4), and thus he became "wroth" (angry, livid). Observe how his "countenance fell." Yes, he had a long face, exposing his depression. He was a bitter man who blamed God for his dilemma and took it out on his brother, Abel. I tell you that anger and depression go together! Wrong responses to trials can create a "monster" within our spirit that will eventually kill us and others.[10]

I cannot stress enough the importance of keeping your heart free from bitterness. It is a cancer that will affect every aspect of your life. As mentioned previously, it is "the little foxes that destroy the vine." The gross, outward sins of the world are not usually the problem with the saints; rather, it's the inner attitudes of fear, worry and resentment. If the Devil can't succeed in destroying your reputation, he will whittle away your spiritual vitality with subtle and wicked thinking. *"For as he* (a man) *thinketh in his heart, so is he"* (Proverbs 23:7). One cannot live any higher than he thinks! What's in the heart will eventually come out in action.

Fainting in Trial

Another possible response to trial is to "faint" or become weary. Note that the writer says don't *"faint when thou art rebuked of him."* (Hebrews 12:5) God in his training program confronts us with truth and correction; how we respond is all important. We need not become faint-hearted nor overwhelmed by the difficulty at hand. In fact, we were

CHAPTER 5: WRONG RESPONSE TO TRIALS

exhorted in verse 3 to consider Christ's suffering on the Cross as an antidote (remedy) to spiritual fainting spells.

Most folks faint at the wrong time. Just when they're needed the most, they quit! I'm thinking of an accident scene on the highway where assistance to the victim(s) is gravely important. I can see one potential helper who is paralyzed by the sight of blood and faints to the pavement. The pressure of the moment overwhelmed this individual, producing a wrong response. Now we have an additional victim instead of another helper!

How the church is filled with fainters who are tired out and have become passive to the claims of Christ upon their lives! *"Most men will proclaim every one his own goodness: but a faithful man who can find?"* said Solomon in Proverbs 20:6. Faithful people are not fainters, but recognize the goodness of God even in His discipline program. *"For whom the Lord loveth he chasteneth, and scourgeth every son whom he receiveth."* (Hebrews 12:6) We are saved on purpose for a purpose, and fainting is not an option.

Endurance in Trial

Going with the flow of God's discipline is the right response—a manifestation of true faith. *"If ye endure chastening, God dealeth with you as with sons..."* (12:7) Our mental attitude regarding our sonship in Christ is all important here. Our loving Father is purposely using trials to develop our growth and maturity. He is training us for the long haul, i.e., the ability to persevere to the end. Therefore, He not only looks at the starting line, but intends that we cross the finish line as well.

The word "endure" is very interesting and expressive. It is the Greek word *hupomeno*, meaning literally to "remain under"; thus to "bear up bravely" or "persevere" under pressure. It depicts the training of a long-distance runner who must persevere under excruciating stress and pain. This is the significance of its usage in 2Timothy 2:10-12, where Paul testifies to young Timothy of his personal endurance of *"all things for the elect's sakes."* He then challenges and encourages Timothy with the promise: *"If we suffer (hupomeno–persevere, endure), we shall also reign with him."* There is definite reward for the saint's faithful perseverance and endurance in obeying the will of God.

After all, was this not the focal point of Hebrews 12:2&3 where the writer challenges the saints to run the race *"with patience"* (*hupomeno*) while *"looking unto Jesus"* who *"endured the cross"*? In other words, Jesus is our ultimate Pioneer of faith, who persevered through the horrendous suffering of the Crucifixion and thus enables us to endure suffering as well. This is all part of the Father's purpose to conform us to the image of His Son (Romans 8:28-30). Prolonged ignorance or misunderstanding of this said purpose is to become disheartened and depressed.

The fruit of the Holy Spirit is not only "love, joy and peace," but also "faith" or faithfulness to God (Galatians 5:22). Paul says: *"Faithful is he that calleth you, who also will do it."* (1Thessalonians 5:24) Faith somehow plugs into the provision of God's enabling grace and thus endures. Faith is not some emotional feeling, but rather the heart's commitment to obey God, and to "keep on keepin' on" when trials come.

Isn't this really the very character of true love that *"beareth all things, believeth all things, hopeth all things, endureth all things?"* (1Corinthians 13:7) Note how love not only believes, but hopes—and thus endures. This sequence is vital, because my hope in the ultimate and future victory of Christ's Kingdom is essential to my present ability to endure. Biblical hope is much different than the world's cliché, "I hope

CHAPTER 5: WRONG RESPONSE TO TRIALS

everything turns out OK." Rather, it is the confident assurance and calm anticipation that all things will come out right in the end because our God reigns! That kind of hope enables me to endure the hardships of daily life. Without this future hope in Christ, who is the Hope of Glory, my present faith and love will begin to wane.[11]

I would think that the three Hebrew children in Daniel 3 knew this principle when confronted with the fiery furnace. Talk about facing a "fiery trial!" These servants of Jehovah were really put to the test when commanded by the king to bow down and worship the golden image. Upon their refusal, they were tied hand and foot and cast into the furnace—now heated seven times hotter. Amazingly, they were preserved in the flames by "the Son of God," who joined them in the fire. The king, looking through the peep hole, saw four men walking in the midst. Perplexed and fearful, he released the three boys who were miraculously unscathed by the flames!

What a testimony of God's faithfulness to His children who endured by faith! In fact, they were not only delivered from the furnace, but didn't even have a singed hair on their heads! The Lord did not keep them from the furnace, but He did preserve them *in* the flames. The Author of their faith met them in the fire, allowing only the ropes that bound them to be burned. Thus they could walk with Jesus, even in that horrendous circumstance!

How this illustrates the faithfulness of God in even the most extreme trials! Seeing that the ropes that had restricted their movement were now removed, they had a unique privilege and experience—freedom to walk with Jesus in the fire! In fact, they had more freedom *in* the furnace of affliction than they had on the outside! How this speaks of God's ability to give perfect peace and deliverance, even in the most overwhelming situations!

I can't resist asking the question, Where is Jesus today? Well, according to Daniel, He's still in the furnace! Remember, there were four inside, and only three came out. It has to be comforting to know that in the "fires" of life, there is still One in the midst to meet us. It might further be said that it's better to be **in** the fiery furnace with Jesus than to be out of the fire without Him. This fact alone should keep us from becoming disheartened and depressed. Moreover, James promises true happiness to those who endure:

> *"Blessed is the man that endureth temptation: for when he is tried, he shall receive the crown of life, which the Lord hath promised to them that love him." (James 1:12)*

Let us learn by faith that our God is using trials to make us like His Son. (Romans 8:29) Thus, we are on a journey of development under the tutelage of our Heavenly Father. Our actions are important, but our reactions are even more important. Knowing His purpose, let us not resent his discipline, nor faint in the midst; but rather let us "endure to the end" in true faith, looking unto Jesus who IS our Hope! Let's become *better*, instead of bitter!

Chapter Six

Lack of Appreciation and Understanding from Others

Another surface cause of depression is our response to the criticism from those we love and serve. We'd all like to think that what people think of us is of no import or concern. But that is just not the case. We do want to have favor with the people to whom we minister; that is just built into our human frame. Every normal person desires to be appreciated. Therefore, how we respond to rejection can greatly affect our spiritual and emotional health.

I have made the following statement to my students: "I don't care what you think of me now, but I do care what you think when we all stand someday before the Lord." I can honestly say that I mean that, but at the same time there's something within that also cares about what they think of me now. I'm somewhat elated and encouraged when they desire to obey the Word; at the same time, I'm disappointed when a student is indifferent or flat-out disobedient. To have all of them reject my ministry (like Ezekiel of old) would be unbearable, naturally speaking.

The problem is that we interpret their rejection as being aimed at us; that is, we take it personally, rather than recognizing their rejection of God and His Word. That can throw us for a spiritual loss! I believe this is an all too common problem among those who minister the Word of God, whether publicly or privately. This is basic in the matter of witnessing, because we fear rejection. Who doesn't want to be liked and appreciated?

Moses' Problem

I think one of the most difficult blows to a sincere leader is when his motives are impugned or misunderstood. After all, this is what triggered Moses' flight from Egypt to Midian after attempting to mediate a dispute between two brethren (Exodus 2:11-15). Moses was aware of the Lord's call upon his life to deliver Israel out of Egypt.

As a grown man, he demonstrated his awareness of this call by extending compassion and vital interest in the condition of the Hebrew people (2:11). In fact, he was quick to defend one brother who was being "smitten" by an Egyptian, resulting in Moses slaying the perpetrator. While many commentators would convict him of Murder One, I believe that Moses saw this act as the beginning of Israel's deliverance "by his hand," that is, through Moses' instrumentality. He truly believed that he was God's ordained liberator for the captives of Israel!

Was he misguided in assuming that he was to take on the Egyptian army single-handed? Was his action premature and presumptuous? Yes, indeed. Was his heart in the right place; i.e., did he fully intend to protect and deliver his brother? Yes, he did. In fact, it was with that attitude that he attempted to mediate between two quarreling brethren on the next day (Exodus 2:13). Upon confronting the wrong-doer, he was met with a barrage of slanderous opposition which devastated Moses (2:14). This soul crisis is captured centuries later in Stephen's sermon:

> *"And when he (Moses) was full forty years old, it came into his heart to visit his brethren the children of Israel. And seeing one of them suffer wrong, he defended him, and avenged him that was oppressed....For he <u>supposed his brethren would have</u>*

CHAPTER 6: LACK OF UNDERSTANDING FROM OTHERS

<u>*understood*</u> *how that God by his hand would deliver them: <u>but they understood not.</u>" (Acts 7:23-25, underline mine)*

How could his brethren ever misunderstand what Moses was doing? But they did, and he couldn't believe it! In fact, he couldn't handle it emotionally and thus fled the scene. Sound familiar? I personally relate to this episode, as do many of you who read these words. How could the brethren ever second-guess our motives when we really had their welfare in mind? Even if our actions were not exactly right, couldn't they see the right intent of our hearts?

There's hardly anything that will discourage a sincere servant any quicker than misunderstanding. We can endure all sorts of trial and difficulty in ministry, but this area seems the most devastating. How many times in personal ministry have we been misjudged by the brethren upon suggesting a new direction or innovation in the work? The difficulty is not so much their questioning of the idea per se, but their judging of the motive behind it.

Moses' intent was right, although his method of performance was wrong. God forgave him even when his brothers did not! That is still difficult to live with, because we want so much to be understood and accepted by those we love. To be rejected here is to be rejected—even if we know that God understands! Why, it's enough to throw one into a "pity party." I guess it shouldn't be that way, but such is the reality of human frailty.

A good piece of advice to Christian leaders is in order here. This was spoken to me years ago, and experience tells me it's true. If you are one step ahead of the flock, you are a leader; if you are two steps ahead, you're a martyr! Moses' vision was "too far out" for the brethren to comprehend, much less follow. Sheep must be led, for sure, but only one step at a time. Moreover, may God pity the pastor who is not only too far out in front, but decides to drive or coerce the flock. That can only be disastrous.

Thank God, our Heavenly Shepherd always leads his sheep. David said:

> *"...He leadeth me beside still waters. He restoreth my soul; He leadeth me in the paths of righteousness for His name's sake..." (Psalm 23:2,3)*

He never drives us—that's what Satan does. A driven leader will only be frustrated and perplexed, thus attempting to force his agenda on the flock. How precious to be led by the Lord, enjoying His presence and wisdom which is then communicated gently to the sheep. How such a leadership attitude is an antidote to distress and burnout!

Taking this even to another level, some leaders get discouraged and disillusioned when not recognized properly by the brethren. In the local church, it might take the form of, "If they loved and appreciated me, they would raise my salary." In the larger realm of Christian organization, it might be stated thusly: "Why is it that I am not recognized by the group and elected moderator? After all, I have served these folks faithfully over the years, and that's the least they could do!" How subtle is the flesh, and its desire to be exalted! How it craves the fleeting plaudits of men!

Solomon exhorted us ably when he said: *"Trust in the LORD with all thine heart; and lean not unto thine own understanding. In all thy ways acknowledge him, and he shall direct thy paths."* (Proverbs 3:5-6) True promotion is of the Lord—not from men. Even in the midst of great trial, the

CHAPTER 6: LACK OF UNDERSTANDING FROM OTHERS

confidence of His direction is constant and sure. This kind of hope goes a long way in remedying the seeds of depression and potential burnout.

PART III

ROOT CAUSES OF DEPRESSION

Chapter Seven

Covetousness

We move now from the surface causes of depression to the root of the matter. One of the fundamental marks of our sin nature is covetousness or a "lusting after that which God forbids or has not allowed us to have." It has been rightly called the "gluttony of the soul." Interestingly, the Scriptures use "covet" in both a good and bad sense. Primarily, it is a strong desire for that which is forbidden and thus sinful. Paul, however, exhorts us to *"covet earnestly the best gifts"* (1Corinthians 12:31); i.e. to be zealous for that which would make our lives more effective for God.

We all have desires, but some are legitimate, and others are not. In fact, if we were filled with the right desires, we would have no room for fleshly lusts. Jesus said, *"Blessed are they which do hunger and thirst after righteousness: for they shall be filled"* (Matthew 5:6). O, to lust after the things of God! As the Psalmist said, *"I stretch forth my hands unto thee: my soul thirsteth after thee, as a thirsty land. Selah."* (Psalm 143:6)

The Peril of Greed

Covetousness is a bed-rock sin resident in every human heart. It's the one commandment that everyone has unquestionably broken. While murder and adultery have been openly committed by some, covetousness is a universal heart condition. Even the apostle Paul testifies in Romans 7:7f, how that the Law of God triggered his consciousness of sin when it said: *"Thou shalt not covet."* This one-time Pharisee, who boasted of his flawless obedience to the precepts of Judaism, now confesses his lustful heart of covetousness.

I believe that covetousness is a stronghold not only in the world, but in the church. Funds for missions are withheld or locked down because of this sin. Because it is a root problem, it can easily go undetected. Worldly activities and sinful habits are quickly observed, but one's greed is not. Desire for money, power, and sex can be well hidden in the heart. For instance, how many believers desire or focus on worldly things, but never follow through because of the risk of being discovered? How many would be first in the food line if it were not interpreted as being unchristian? I'm talking about the depth of sinfulness.

Sorry to say, this malady is not just prevalent in the pew, but also in the pulpit. Anyone who has moved in ecclesiastical circles knows how preachers can play politics. Jockeying for position and money is not uncommon. Not only is this true in denominational and fellowship groups, but in the local church itself. How many pastors and musicians are discouraged because their remuneration is so minimal compared with those in the secular world? Instead of committing their finances to the Lord, claiming the promise of God's provision (Matthew 6:33), they envy the world and secretly lust for riches. Needless to say, this may well account for such a lack of spiritual power in the ministry.

Asaph's Conflict

The Scripture gives a prime example of this problem in the person of Asaph, King David's worship leader. His personal testimony is recorded in Psalm 73, where Asaph uniquely describes his bout with depression. An abbreviated study of this narrative affords us a clear understanding of depression—its cause and cure.

This godly praise leader candidly shares his personal struggle and its effect.[12] He reveals to us what happens when

CHAPTER 7: LACK OF UNDERSTANDING FROM OTHERS

we lose our spiritual focus and become myopic or self-absorbed. Asaph exclaims in Psalm 73:1-3:

> *"Truly God is good to Israel, even to such as are of a clean heart. But as for me, my feet were almost gone; my steps had well nigh slipped. For I was envious at the foolish, when I saw the prosperity of the wicked."*

See how accurate and definite is Asaph's theology! "God is good!" Isn't that the Bible "cheer" that resounds in churches across the world each week? Certainly, "God is good all the time," we say—yet do we really believe it? David's worship leader, like the rest of us, had a deep conflict between what he knew to be true and what he was actually experiencing. Somehow his head was on a different channel than his heart.

He knew the right words: "God is good." However, his conflict is revealed when he adds, *"But as for me, my feet were almost gone; my steps had well nigh slipped."* In one breath, he's expressing God's great goodness to Israel, while in the next he describes his defeat. Yes, God is good—BUT as for me...! How the "but" changes things.

I assume that Asaph was regularly leading that great congregation in praise and worship, extolling the goodness of his God; yet he pictures himself as one who has "one foot in the grave, and the other on a banana peel." His solid position of praise has become a slippery slope due to a sinful attitude. He reveals the reason for his dilemma in verse 3: *"For* (because) *I was envious at the foolish* (arrogant boasters)*, when I saw the prosperity of the wicked."* His eyes have somehow become focused on the material world, leaving him depressed. His praise to God now has become just lip service.

Covetousness is so subtle. It's a matter of perspective because every true believer is rich in Christ. But Asaph honestly expresses his envy for the wicked, who evidently were prospering in a way he was not. After all, wasn't he the servant of God? Why should the godless be wealthy when they blaspheme Jehovah—by life and lip? This whole scenario develops into a full-blown issue with God Himself.

I think it is significant that Asaph continues in his ministry of worship leader in spite of his conflict. I don't believe he was guilty of the more visible sins of adultery, drunkenness, vagrancy, and the like. Rather, he was greatly disturbed on the inside, where it couldn't be initially detected. Great leaders have fallen in open sin, like David himself. But there are many more who suffer from hidden sin while continuing to go through the motions of ministry. "O yes, God is good—*but* as for me...!"

Indeed, it is the "little foxes that spoil the vines." If the enemy can't get a leader to fall into open sin, he'll encourage the "little sins" like covetousness and resentment, which eat away at the roots of the soul. As we have stated previously, little foxes can't reach the grapes, so they slowly eat away at the vine's roots, eventually destroying the vineyard. It's one thing to eat the grapes, it's another to devour the root system, preventing any future production. How subtle is that!

The Wicked Described

Asaph begins to enumerate the character traits of the wicked as seen through his own faulty vision. "Look at their prosperity, will you?" There are *"no bands* (bonds) *in their death; but their strength is firm."* (Psalm 73:4) They don't seem to be *"in trouble as other men."* (vs.5) They're filled with *"pride* and *violence"* (vs.6), and yet *"they have more than heart could wish"* (abundance). They *"increase in riches"*

CHAPTER 7: LACK OF UNDERSTANDING FROM OTHERS

(vs.12), while they live in rebellion against God.

The psalmist is in deep conflict of soul as he tries to interpret the status of the ungodly around him. He envies their prosperity, especially in light of their wicked condition. How could God allow this to happen? If I'm serving the Lord, why doesn't He prosper me more than they? This really isn't fair! And so the reasoning goes.

But is what Asaph sees the reality of it all? Does his covetous spirit color or distort the truth? If he could actually witness the wicked at death's door, would they be as strong and carefree as he intimates? Are they really trouble free, or is that the way it appears when you look through covetous eyes? The fact is that the world lives on Fantasy Island and all their prosperity is fleeting and unsatisfying. This is as close to Heaven as they will ever get, apart from God's saving grace! Thank God, Asaph eventually sees this fact.

It must be stated here that the Psalmist is right about the pride and arrogance of the wicked. In fact, along with his envy regarding their prosperity, he is resentful that God has somehow "rewarded" their wickedness. This viewpoint really exacerbates the covetousness. For now he has a further issue with God, who would allow such prosperity to those who hate Him. At the same time, why would those who love God be allowed to continue on the so-called poverty level?

This looks like the wicked live trouble free, while true saints of God are hard pressed to make it in this world. The ungodly are allowed to do their thing, while believers are tested and tried at every turn of life! Isn't there something wrong with this picture? There is, if you're looking through your own eyes, as was Asaph. Jesus said, *"In the world ye shall have tribulation: but be of good cheer; I have overcome the world"* (John 16:33). Asaph had to find the key to overcoming grace, and so must we.

A Radical Conclusion

In the midst of his bout with covetousness and disillusionment, the Psalmist makes an almost unbelievable statement: *"Verily, I have cleansed my heart in vain, and washed my hands in innocency."* (73:13) What's that, Asaph? Are you saying that it was no use to be cleansed and forgiven of sin through the sacrifice? You mean, you didn't know what you were doing when you came to Jehovah for salvation? It was all just blind faith, and of no account?

Wow! This admission is comparable to the New Testament saint saying, "I got saved for nothing! What's the use of being born again?" Asaph's reason: *"For all the day long have I been plagued* (literally, stricken), *and chastened* (punished or rebuked) *every morning."* (vs.14) In other words, I thought the Christian life is one of victory and abundance; why am I daily under such a load of difficulty? One problem leads to another. Somehow this doesn't wash with my concept of serving God.

I submit that this conflict is commonplace in the inner spirit of many servants of God. It is not vocalized and squarely faced, like Asaph's confession, but aren't you glad that someone had the courage to spell it out, even in Holy Scripture? In fact, he readily sensed the serious consequences and pain of such an outburst when he says, *"If I...speak thus...I should offend...thy children."* (vs.15) He recognizes that such unbelief on his part could easily cause the younger saints to stumble. Isn't that also our concern when we have become depressed and defeated?

The Turning Point

Thank God for a man who tells it like it is, revealing his actual experience. Likewise, I'm thankful that he progresses

CHAPTER 7: LACK OF UNDERSTANDING FROM OTHERS

out of that state of mind. The turning point comes in 73:17 where he enters God's sanctuary. There his mind and spiritual eyes are refocused. He runs, as it were, into the presence of God, where now his 20/20 vision is restored. He cries, *"Then I understood their* (wicked) *end."* He now sees the fate of the ungodly from God's perspective.

While Asaph had described himself as having no solid footing (vs.2), he now comprehends that it is really the wicked who are in *"slippery places."* (vs.18) Yes, they will be *"brought into desolation"* and *"utterly consumed with terrors."* (vs.19) He recognizes that the Lord is Just and all things will come out right. Consequently, there is no reason to envy the wicked, as though they are getting away with something. None will escape the justice of God!

The goodness of God's revelation leads the Psalmist to repentance. He sees himself now through God's eyes rather than his own. His heart is broken and he confesses his foolishness and ignorance regarding the ways of God (73:21, 22). He is confronted with his perverted spiritual perspective and cries, *"I was as a beast before thee."* That is, I've been as an animal, devoid of any spiritual life and understanding.

Evidently, this sin of envy is considered a serious issue before the Lord. I can hear someone blame Asaph's problem on some "mental illness." That seems to be a common justification of sin in our day. But, thank God, the Psalmist comes to grip with an enormous cancer of the soul and deals with it accordingly! No copping out of his responsibility. No pills, medication, or so-called therapy to cover up the symptoms; rather he goes to the root of the problem—sinful, selfish thinking. It is imperative that we do the same.

Hope Restored

I cannot stress enough the importance of Asaph's actions here. His deliverance from depression results from his repentance of this envy and unbelief. Note that he makes no excuses for his condition—no blaming of others or "passing the buck," as we say. Rather he faces squarely his own responsibility in the matter. Thus he reaps the glorious result of renewed hope in the Lord.

Briefly stated, he now once again revels in the sense of God's presence and security (vs.23). His confidence in the Lord's guidance and hope for future glory is renewed (vs.24). His outburst of praise for the Lord's strength and the promise of eternal inheritance is contagious (vs.26)! Last, but not least, he concludes, *"It is good for me to draw near to God."* (vs.28) Now after this horrendous bout with depression he verifies what he said up front: *"Truly God is good"* (vs.1). In other words, he proclaims that it is a "good thing to draw near to the Good God!"

How relevant is this Psalm for our day! I'm so glad that Asaph's testimony is in the Bible. This pattern of remedy over depression is critical in a time when such problems are relegated to mental illness and thus "treated" with psychotropic (mind altering) medication. We will further explore this subject later.

Chapter Eight

Unbelief

A Matter of Life or Death

Probably the most basic root cause of depression is unbelief. This is closely linked with covetousness and is often found even in the believer's life. It can be said that an unbelieving spirit is the fundamental sin of all mankind because it denies who Jesus Christ really is. He said in John 6:47: *"Verily, verily, I say unto you, He that believeth on me hath everlasting life."* Belief or faith in Christ is a matter of life and death!

To the Christian, faith is a matter of victory or defeat, courage or discouragement, even spiritual sanity or insanity. Unbelief is our failure to take God at His word, which can only stifle and short-circuit His power in our lives. In fact, unbelief is really a slander against the character of God Himself! This is why Asaph's covetous spirit was so lethal. He was doubting the goodness of God. Therefore, out of unbelief flow all kinds of sinful attitudes and actions.

The Scripture states: *"...without faith it is impossible to please him; for he that cometh to God must believe that he is, and that he is a rewarder of them that diligently seek him."* (Hebrews 11:6) We are exhorted here to believe God for all that He is. Unbelief looks away from God and focuses on self. That is the essence of sin. In fact, that was Lucifer's problem in Heaven when he revolted against God's sovereign rule. It's called pride.

The Garden of Eden

It must be said here that unbelief is an attitude of pride, more than an overt action. Certainly Lucifer, who became

Satan, was not kicked out of Heaven for drug abuse or drunkenness—but because of sinful pride.[13] Thus, all the "big" sins like stealing, murder, and adultery begin with pride and unbelief. In Genesis 3, we have the historical record of how sin entered the human race.

Our original ancestors, Adam and Eve, were placed in the beautiful Garden of Eden. They had all their heart could desire, not the least of which was fellowship with the God who made them. The one test to their faith was God's prohibition regarding the tree of the knowledge of good and evil. Every other tree in the garden was at their disposal, but this tree had to do with the Lord's purpose in distinguishing between the creature and his Creator. Adam's mind was to be subjected to God, lest he become a sinful rebel against the knowledge of God, as did Lucifer.

Wouldn't you know that the Devil, as a deceitful serpent, takes advantage of the first couple regarding this prohibition! It's like he was saying: "If I couldn't make it in Heaven, these folks will not have the blessing of God either—if I can help it." Thus, his very first attack is focused on their belief or trust in the veracity of the Word of God. Very subtly the Devil says, *"Yea, hath God said, Ye shall not eat of every tree of the garden?"* In other words, do you really believe God's Word? Satan's tactic hasn't changed from that day to this!

I think it is significant to observe the seeming innocence of their sin. What could be so bad about eating a piece of fruit from a tree? And really, was that the primary sin or was it the outward expression of something within? I submit that they sinned before ever eating the fruit—it was the unbelief of their hearts. It is almost like God made the outward sin to appear somewhat harmless, so as to demonstrate that sin is primarily a matter of the heart.

CHAPTER 8: UNBELIEVE

Taking God at His Word is still the primary issue today. The first couple yielded to the enemy's temptation to disobey the clear command of God, and the rest is a tragic history. Unbelief is the bedrock sin of humanity. Isaiah states this precept clearly: *"All we like sheep have gone astray; we have turned every one to his own way..."* (53:6) Out of our "own way" (pride, unbelief) flows all kinds of sin and corruption.[14] Adam and Eve had a choice to go their way, or God's. Obviously they made the wrong choice. That choice is still relevant today, even in the life of a Christian.

It might be said that unbelief is slandering the character of God. When we fail to take Him at His Word, we deny who He is. For instance, God is good, regardless what I may feel or experience. As he did with the first couple, Satan continues to do with us—to slander God. "How can God be good," he says, "if He allows so many bad things to happen in your life?" Remember, he is the accuser by trade, the anti-Christ, and will do his best to talk us out of a stalwart faith in the true God.

Suffice to say, that if the enemy can successfully get us to question or deny God's goodness, we are headed toward the slough of depression. It is essential, therefore, to live in an attitude of praise to the Faithful One, even when we can't sense His presence. That's what David did in Psalm 42:5 when faced with a depressive spirit. *"Why art thou cast down, O my soul? ...hope thou in God: for I shall yet praise him for the help of his countenance."*

He declared his faith and hope in God, though he was pressed down. He talked to himself on the basis of the Word— what he knew to be God's character. Thus, he "caught himself" in unbelief, taking drastic measures to recover. He refused to continue being controlled by his feelings, thus standing by faith on the revealed character of God's goodness. So must we.

Chapter Nine

Resentment toward God

Cain's "Dis-ABEL-ment"

I believe that the first Biblical example of depression is found in the life of Cain (Genesis 4). We remember Cain for two reasons: 1) He was the first baby born into the world; and 2) He killed his brother Abel. This episode speaks volumes! How could there possibly be such wickedness so early in human history? What could have driven Cain to commit such a dastardly deed?

It's mind-boggling to think that the first child in history was a murderer. How bizarre is that? A cookie-thief, maybe, but not a cold-blooded killer! Right up front in Scripture we have a revelation of the indescribable depth of human depravity—a primary example of Jeremiah's axiom: *"The heart is deceitful above all things, and desperately wicked: who can know it?"*[14]

What could ever possess Cain to do such a thing? Let's take a brief look at the situation. Here are two brothers who grew up in a near-perfect environment, taught and reared by the same parents. Abel went with the teaching, but Cain didn't. Abel obeyed the Lord in bringing a lamb as his offering. Cain brought his own offering—some produce from the ground.

A Case of Divine Injustice?

Keep in mind that the lamb's sacrifice was revealed to Adam and Eve, who were clothed by the Lord in skin (Genesis 3:21). It's safe to assume that Cain and Abel were both exposed to this principle by their parents. But Cain took offense and became livid when God didn't accept his offering.

It says specifically that *"Cain was very wroth, and his countenance* (face) *fell."* Isn't that the typical symptom of depressed people, who are both angry and sad? We have here the reason behind the "long face."

Note how Cain deals with the situation. Rather than taking God's gracious offer to return with a lamb (Genesis 4:7), he decides to murder his brother and present him as a rebellious blood sacrifice! This same murderous spirit has flowed down through every generation. Even the religious hierarchy of Jesus' day was rebuked when He said, *"Ye are of your father the devil, and the lusts of your father ye will do. He was a murderer from the beginning, and abode not in the truth, because there is no truth in him."* (John 8:44)

I bring this up because even in a believer's life, although a new creature in Christ, there is still a struggle in regard to lying and murder. While outward habits may be quick to change, inner attitudes die hard. It's still difficult to face the truth about ourselves, along with escaping resentment and bitterness toward others. I know personally that it is possible to carry past grudges and hurt feelings into the Christian life.

More specifically, a Christian can take issue with God Himself, just as Cain did. How many saints have questioned God's call upon their lives or allowed things to happen which could not be understood nor accepted? How many times have we said in essence, "It's not fair!" How many prayers have we offered about a certain thing that never came to pass? "Where were you, Lord?" How many people have stepped on us, and we hate them? Then we resent God too for letting it happen. These are very real attitudes that rarely are faced squarely and Biblically.

No wonder even believers turn to the mental health community for help. Tranquilizers of all sorts are the rage even

CHAPTER 9: RESENTMENT TOWARD GOD

among church folks. In fact, many physical ailments, like ulcers, colitis, etc. can result from resentment.[15] Good health, physically and spiritually, is not so much a matter of what you eat, but "what eats you!" An unforgiving spirit will "kill" you, making you unfruitful and powerless. In a word, constantly getting "burned up" will eventually lead to our getting "burned out!"

Chapter Ten

Hopelessness

The last root cause of depression which I will mention is hopelessness. There is hardly anything more devastating than losing hope in the midst of a hopeless world. Depression is epidemic in our country, where ironically, material riches abound. Never have we had so much, but never have we had so little! The love of money is king, even in a vast number of churches. Somehow we have lost our way, and hope in our Saviour has been lost in the shuffle.

Hope has to do with living with eternity in view, as opposed to living for the moment. The great emphasis today, in and out of the church, is how to be happy, healthy and rich. Sermons and seminars are replete with "self-esteem" issues, attempting to make this present existence more palatable. The Gospel has been hijacked by false prophets to build man's kingdom instead of God's.

Consequently, faith has been relegated to "naming and claiming" what I need to be happy. Love, in the human realm, has likewise been perverted to sensuality and lust. "I can't wait," says the lustful man, "I must have it now!" Even God's character of love has been misinterpreted to mean that He overlooks man's lost condition and gladly receives unrepentant sinners. But John 3:16 says:

> *"For God so loved the world that He gave his only begotten Son; that whosoever believeth on him shall not perish, but have everlasting life."*

Yes! God so loved the world—but it doesn't stop there. God's love made a way through the Cross for man's sin to be paid, thus satisfying God's justice. Sinful man has no standing whatsoever before a Holy God! Christ alone is "the Way, the Truth, and the Life," and none can get to Heaven apart from Him! (John 14:6)

Ignorance and misunderstanding in these areas of Biblical faith and love can only be spiritually disastrous. The present man-centered teachings on self-esteem, happy feelings, and personal prosperity will not enhance the believer's stability in light of hardships and persecution. No one finds happiness by searching for it; it comes as a result of choosing to follow Christ, no matter what! But, as we shall see next, the key ingredient to making faith and love effective and lasting is Biblical hope.

True faith and love have to do with the believer's obedience to God and His Word, resulting in ministry to others. Paul makes this clear in his commendation of the young believers at Thessalonica. I remember *"without ceasing,"* he says, *"your work of faith, and labor of love, and patience of hope in our Lord Jesus Christ..."* (1Thessalonians 1:3). They had a faith that worked, a love that labored, but not without a hope than endured. This is a key issue if we are to understand how depression creeps into our minds.

Hope in the Scripture has nothing to do with the wishful expressions of our modern day. It's often said, "I hope everything turns out alright," or "I hope so." These fall far short of true hope in God. Such platitudes only further demonstrate man's hopeless desperation.

Biblical hope can be defined as that calm anticipation of the Lord's return in glory when all will be made right. It is that assuring confidence in the believer's soul that God is on the throne of the universe and will judge all things in His time. It's the "anchor" of future hope that motivates us in this present world.

CHAPTER 10: HOPELESSNESS

Faith, then, is the ability to trust God in the present tense because of a steadfast hope in the Lord of the future. Take away that hope, and our faith ceases to work; take away that hope, and our love begins to wane. Paul cites these believers who demonstrated the present effectiveness of their faith and love, enabled by the persevering grace of future hope! Could it be said that hope is the "super-glue" that holds faith and love together? Remove that "cement" and the faith and love become dysfunctional.

Now you know why pastors, missionaries, and other workers leave their posts. When hope wanes, so does the ability to continue to believe God and love the people. Christians in all walks of life are suffering major defeat for the same reason. Whatever robs us of our steadfast hope in God will debilitate our effectiveness in the present. Often this leads one to pursue selfish and material gain to offset growing depression. This, in turn, can only lead to further disillusionment and spiritual disaster.

It is no wonder that the average Christian is looking for artificial means of pleasure and happiness. God and His Word are no longer sufficient; we have turned to the world for our entertainment. If the truth were known, even our "high-powered" so-called worship services are subtly geared for the pleasures of the flesh. This is not to mention the increasing number of saints who depend on psychotropic medication, i.e. tranquilizers and other mind-altering drugs, to live a "normal" existence.

Something is radically wrong with this picture. Indeed, there must be a solution to such a widespread epidemic. The remainder of this book is dedicated to such. May God be pleased to reveal Himself to each of us as we seek to remedy these causes of depression.

PART IV

THE REMEDY FOR DEPRESSION

Chapter Eleven

Why Drugs Don't Work

In handling this complex subject, I do not want to appear crass by citing simplistic remedies. But let it be said that the Word of God is indeed sufficient and qualified to address the issue. I refuse to concede that the mental health "experts" have the proper understanding of, or remedy for, this vast epidemic of depression. God gave us a "Manual" to go with His product—man; he did not leave us without instructions and the capability to "troubleshoot" when things don't work right. What a source of encouragement and hope is this fact!

In further addressing this issue, Dave Hunt states:

> "Believers throughout the ages have found God's word and His remedies sufficient in every situation. Why turn to pitiful and destructive theories invented by humanists who can't help themselves? Psychologists and psychiatrists have the highest percentage of any profession under the care of psychiatrists, committing suicide, divorcing, and on prescription drugs. Consulting them is like asking directions of someone who is himself hopelessly lost."[16]

Drugs Cannot Reach the Root Problem

Before getting into specific Biblical remedies for depression, it seems fitting to explain why drugs fail as a cure for this problem. Understanding man's makeup is essential to the remedy of depression. The evolutionary hypothesis, upon which medical science is based, has no real clue as to depression's cause or cure. If we started as a "piece of *goo*, ending up in the *zoo*, and now it's *you*"—then who are we, really? Where did we come from? Do we have any self-worth? Can we change for the better? Where are we headed?

These are puzzling questions unless you believe the Biblical account of man's creation. Indeed, the theory of evolution takes more "faith" to believe than what Moses says in Genesis 2:7:

> *"And the LORD God formed man of the dust of the ground, and breathed into his nostrils the breath of life; and man became a living soul."*

Contained in this statement is the remarkable origin of man as a direct creation of God. It is not the writer's purpose here to expound the details and veracity of this act of God.[17] Suffice to say, that man is made up of three parts: body, soul, and spirit. His body was formed of the "dust," thus his name Adam (meaning "ground"). All the minerals and elements in man's body are found in the earth; that is why at death we return to the ground from where we came.

While the body is our physical and tangible part, we also have an intangible function—namely, the soul, which is comprised of will, mind, and emotions. By intangible, we mean untouchable and unseen. The human brain is a physical organ located in the body (head) and can be touched by a neurosurgeon's hand. The mind, however, is a soul function which cannot be ministered to physically. It is beyond the human touch.

This distinction is vital to understanding how humans function and why the consumption of psychotropic drugs are ineffective to cure our so-called mental illnesses. Taking medication for diabetes, hypertension, and the like, is effective because it ministers to a physical, bodily condition. Prozac, on the other hand, is taken orally, and though it affects the brain and body, it cannot reach the real problem, namely the mind. We cannot live any higher than we think, and that is deeper than our brain function.

In addition to the soul, we have a spirit or heart that is estranged from God at birth. Jeremiah describes our soul and spirit as follows: *"The heart is deceitful above all things, and desperately wicked* (literally, incurable); *who can know it?"* (Jeremiah 17:9) It is not primarily our I.Q. or intellect that is faulty, but our minds that are defiled by sin.[18] Therefore, drugs cannot reach deeply enough to affect or change that part of us. While the physician can operate on our brain, he cannot treat our mind (soul). In fact, nothing in this world can cure a human mind—that is only reserved for God and His Word!

This fact alone is fundamental in dealing with the primary cause of depression. This is the missing element in so-called mental health remedies. May I say boldly that this fact alone is revolutionary in our modern day, when even Christian leaders have traded in the Bible for a psychological "mess" of pottage! We have surrendered the Truth to a system based, at best, on humanistic suppositions. It is here that the conflict between evolution and creationism is most acute.

Drugs May Be the Problem!

Lest the reader accuse the writer of Christian bias, let us consider some observations coming from the secular world. For instance, in his book *Your Drug May Be Your Problem,* psychiatrist Dr. Peter R. Breggin challenges the whole mental health community with some relevant information. Asking the question: "What is your ultimate resource?" he argues that everyone turns to someone or something when feeling emotionally upset and hopeless. The issue is how do we deal with these times?

While some turn to loved ones, counselors, hobbies, nature, pets, sports, etc., others "turn to psychoactive or mind-altering substances. Although they may believe or hope that they are relying on seemingly objective science, in reality they are placing their faith in drug company marketing—and so are their doctors."[19]

Dr. Breggin further states, regarding seeking relief:

> "If people do feel better when drinking alcohol or smoking marijuana, it is because they feel better when their brain is impaired. Psychiatric drugs are no different. The people who take such drugs may feel less of their emotional suffering. They may even reach a state of relative anesthesia. But to the degree that they feel better, it is because they are experiencing intoxication with the drugs."[20]

It must be said that Dr. Breggin is only one of an increasing number of medical authorities who are alarmed by the deluge and corresponding abuse of antidepressant drugs. Dr. Alan Inglis M.D., affectionately called "America's Country Doctor," takes issue with what he perceives as the "shady tactics" of drug companies. This is an additional arena of concern.

A group of researchers has compared the published results of antidepressant drug producers with The Federal Drug Administration's (FDA) review of the same. The published studies tended to present a "rosy" picture, showing 94 percent of the results to be positive. However, when the researchers

CHAPTER 11: WHY DRUGS DON'T WORK

compared this version with the FDA's numbers, only 51 percent of the results were positive! There's something wrong with this picture.

In light of the above observation, along with other issues of integrity regarding drug companies, Dr. Inglis exhorts:

> "If you're suffering from depression, this means that you and your doctor are trying to make a treatment decision in the dark. With access only to inaccurate information, (what I like to call 'lies'), treating depression becomes a game of Russian roulette. Your doctor relies on the information from these studies to make the best decision for you, in hopes of providing you a true positive outcome. That's a challenging task if he isn't given all of the facts—much less the truth."[21]

Dr. Breggin makes some additional and provoking comments on what we should learn through suffering:

> "Emotional suffering is inevitable in life. But it has a meaning—a purpose. Suffering is a signal that life matters. Specifically, it is usually a signal that something in our lives that matters a great deal needs to be addressed. Depression, guilt, anxiety, shame, chronic anger, emotional numbing—all of these reactions signal that something is amiss and requires special attention. The depth of suffering is a sign of the soul's desire for a better, more creative, more principled life."[22]

These are phenomenal observations, especially from a secular psychiatrist. Note the thread of human responsibility and accountability that runs through these statements. Would to God such insights were more prevalent in the so-called therapy of Christian counselors! I'm amazed at the common sense approach of some secular counselors, while so many Christian "professionals" seem devoid of godly wisdom and discernment.

The documentation opposing the usage of psychotropic drugs like Prozac, Ritalin, or Xanax, is abundant and growing. This is a vast subject all of its own—too much for this brief discourse. But I need to mention one other area which is frequently given as a cause of depression; i.e. chemical imbalance, so-called. The theory is that the neurotransmitters of the brain cells become dysfunctional, triggering chemical imbalance and subsequent "mental disorder."

No one would argue that our bodies can affect our moods and emotional outlook. But is chemical imbalance a cause or effect of depression? Does the "imbalance" trigger the depression or does "stinkin' thinkin'" influence chemical breakdown? Granted, it's certainly easier to maintain a positive attitude when in healthy physical condition. Anything from a cold to insufficient sleep can affect our moods.

"However, doctors commonly give people psychiatric drugs without checking for obvious signs of serious physical disorder, such as hypothyroidism, estrogen deficiency, or head injury.... Moreover, they seem particularly prone to overlooking the importance of physical symptoms in women. Some women with obvious signs of a hormonal disorder or heart condition are put on antidepressants and antianxiety

CHAPTER 11: WHY DRUGS DON'T WORK

> drugs without first being required by their internists or psychiatrist to undergo a physical evaluation."[23]

It must be said here that depressed people have definite reasons for how they feel. That's why it's imperative to start with a complete physical exam before delving into psychological or emotional disorders. Physical problems certainly can greatly affect one's mental condition and outlook on life. But as I have stressed in this book, there are events and causes for depression that go beyond some virus or disease floating in the air. Even if one should have an undetected biochemical imbalance, there is still no reason "to give them drugs like Prozac or Xanax that cause biochemical imbalances and disrupt brain function."[24]

In fact, there doesn't seem to be any laboratory technique for measuring the actual levels of neurotransmitters in the brain cells. Thus, all the talk about biochemical imbalances has amounted to guesswork. Research in no way fosters the idea that these imbalances are corrected by psychiatric drugs.

> "Rather, it shows that psychiatric drugs create imbalances. In modern psychiatric treatment, we take the single most complicated known creation in the universe—the human brain—and pour drugs into it in the hope of 'improving' its function when in reality we are disrupting its function."[25]

Dear friend, if you should be on anti-depressant medication, please consider the following advice. Don't do anything drastic, but ponder and apply the precepts set forth in this book. Do **not** abruptly withdraw from the medication; first consider having a medical examination to establish your physical well-being. As you begin to conquer your battles with anxiety, resentment, and depression, then you can prayerfully, wisely, and gradually wean yourself from the mind-altering medication. Only you yourself before God will know when the time is right.

Chapter Twelve

The Starting Point

So what is the remedy for the depression? The solution begins in the understanding and application of Hebrews 4:12:

> *"For the word of God is quick, and powerful, and sharper than any two-edged sword; piercing even to the dividing asunder of soul and spirit, and of the joints and marrow; and is a discerner of the thoughts and intents of the heart."*

There is not a neurosurgeon in the world that can operate on the mind! At best, he can open the skull and work on the brain, but never the mind. In other words, man is helpless when it comes to reaching his root problem—an ungodly mind. There is not a drug available, legal or illegal, that can remedy this condition.

If that's the case, then what are we to do? Well, we might consider what God has to say, even though it is considered outmoded and unscientific. The fact is that apart from "divine surgery" there is no hope to heal the root cause of man's dilemma. Let us take a moment to ponder the passage just quoted.

The writer states that *"the word of God is quick* (alive) *and powerful* (or effective)*, and sharper than any two-edged sword, piercing even to the dividing asunder of soul and spirit...."* It takes the living God and His living Word to resurrect a dead soul! While he may have physical life in the body, an unbeliever has no inner life in God; that is, he is dead or separated from Christ who is Life. Jesus didn't come to give folks a new religion, but rather to grant them abundant life. He said in John 10:10:

> *"The thief cometh not, but for to steal, and to kill, and to destroy: I am come that they might have life, and that they might have it more abundantly."*

The context of John's gospel here indicates that Satan is a master-deceiver, robbing and destroying souls that would embrace the truth as it is in Christ. He (Satan) uses false religionists to convince people that there's another "way" to Heaven other than through Jesus' finished Cross-work. A sinner is "dead," meaning he is separated from the life of God, thus, he can do nothing, religiously or otherwise, to produce eternal or abundant life. This life is only found in Christ alone!

By the same token, only God's Word can penetrate the soul and spirit of a human being. What a glorious and hope-filled truth is this fact! The Word, as a double-edged sword (or scalpel) can minister to the root cause of man's dilemma as nothing else can. *"The law* (or Word) *of the Lord is perfect, converting the soul,"* David said. Only a perfect Word can make alive and perfect a sinful, depraved soul!

Furthermore, the Word probes the very secrets and thoughts of the heart or spirit. It "discerns" or evaluates our "intents" or motives. Indeed, God's Word gets to the very heart of the matter, initiating conviction and even healing to the innermost recesses of our being. There is no physician or medication that can begin to reach this area of the human psyche (mind). To seek the healing of our minds through mere psychology and/or psychiatry is at best an exercise in futility.

How tragic that we have a whole nation that has been invaded by drug dependency. Even more tragic is the

CHAPTER 12: THE STARTING POINT

horrendous usage of psychotropic medications, like Prozac, within the church. Evidently, from Christian leaders on down, we have been led to embrace the mental health community as a bona fide healer of the mind! I believe this to be a subtle and deceptive move of the enemy to undermine the unique ministry of the Word in making us mentally sound.

As one who contemplated suicide as a young pastor, I'm so thankful to this day for God's wondrous deliverance from depression and fear through the truth of 2 Timothy 1:7 which reads: *"For God hath not given us the spirit of fear; but of power, and of love, and of a sound mind."* What liberation filled my heart when it dawned on me that salvation through the Cross-work of Christ included the saving and deliverance of my mind! Hallelujah!

Let me close this chapter with an encouraging word to those presently taking "psychiatric" medication. God is greater than your problem and can "break through" the meds and bring deliverance. Sometimes the side-effects will serve to "help" an individual regain his or her "humanness" by boosting the Serotonin level of the brain; in turn, this may enable the believer to recognize and apply Scriptural remedies. This statement may generate further inquiry, but I know whereof I speak. Take hope, my friend, for God is faithful and well able to meet you where you are!

Chapter Thirteen

Coming to a Moment of Truth

As we consider the remedy of depression, it is imperative that a person faces the truth squarely. This is probably the most difficult step in the whole process of healing. Our natural inclination is to deny any guilt or responsibility in the matter. Especially is this true when the mental professionals have convinced us that we have a legitimate "disease." Let me quickly interject that depression will likely cause much "dis-ease" of one sort or another, but we must focus on its source if genuine healing is to come.

Prayerfully Taking Personal Responsibility

At this juncture, it might be well to spend a season of prayer, seeking God for wisdom and clear direction. David prayed:

> "Search me, O, God, and know my heart; try me, and know my thoughts; and see if there be any wicked way in me, and lead me in the way everlasting." (Psa. 139:23, 24)

Notice that David didn't offer to do the "searching" himself, recognizing the possible deception of his heart. God must do the searching with His all-seeing eye, revealing David's true condition. The king was dead serious about having a right relationship with his God. That's an essential factor in dealing affectively with depression.

Could it be, my friend, that you've been resentful or bitter toward someone who offended you? Might it be just an unbelieving heart, failing to take God at His word? How about giving place to Satan's accusations of your past sins, and thus doubting God's forgiveness? Such prolonged thinking can cause depression. Paul says, *"Whatsoever is not of faith is sin."* Let's address these issues head on without making excuses. John says, *"If we (believers) confess our sins, he is faithful and just to forgive us our sins, and to cleanse us from all unrighteousness."* (1John 1:9)

We certainly do not use this strategy with cancer, heart disease, or diabetes, since there are no moral implications inferred. This is not to say, however, that depression may not accompany one's experience of surgery or other chronic physical conditions; but it is possible to suffer horrendous bodily afflictions and still maintain a sweet, trusting spirit in the Lord. The great temptation then is to blame our bitter circumstance on others (family, nationality, economics, disease, etc.) and, yes, even God Himself. After all, isn't that what Adam did in Eden when confronted by the Lord after having eaten the forbidden fruit? He said: "It was the woman *you* gave me!" It wasn't enough that he blamed his wife; He actually held God responsible for the tragedy! After all, wasn't this marriage thing God's idea to begin with?

Believe it or not, my friend, this scenario has not changed one bit since Eden. People still "pass the buck" and then wonder why their lives never change. We all desire the "warm and fuzzy" approach so prevalent today. The "self-esteem" gospel that preaches "I'm OK, you're OK" will not do the job! We must address the root problem of sin and unbelief. Let's put away "pop psychology" and self-centered "spirituality," for it's not about us—it's about Him (Christ)!

A Renewed Mind

Solomon said, *"For as he (man) thinketh in his heart (mind), so is he."* A person cannot live any higher than he thinks. To focus on evil is to do evil things. To be filled with

CHAPTER 13: COMING TO A MOMENT OF TRUTH

righteousness is to do right. It's no surprise that sex offenders are obsessed with pornographic materials. The sinful (unsaved) mind is "possessed" by sin, self, and the world system. But Christ came to deliver us from sin, which includes a renewed mind, i.e. a mind that can now focus on God and His Word! (cf. 2Tim. 1:7; 1Cor. 2:16; Rom. 12:1,2; Phil. 2:5) We can *think* differently because we *are* uniquely different in Christ (2Cor. 5:17)!

Simply put, when Christ died on the Cross he "nailed" all of our sins there with Him (cf. Col. 2:14); by paying the full price (judgment) for our sins, He could now give us His righteousness in return. This is called "justification by faith," i.e. when God looks at the believer in Christ He doesn't see his sin, but rather the perfect righteousness of His Son Jesus! He took my sin, and I take His righteousness—how wonderful is that? That is called the "exchanged life" which characterizes the believer's true position in saving grace. We are no longer under the "condemnation of the law" but under a new law of the "Spirit of life in Christ Jesus." (cf. Rom. 8:1, 2) With a new mind in Christ, we begin to think like God thinks according to His Word (the Bible). Now we can deal properly with life's challenges, handling them in a godly fashion. We can "pray in the Spirit," with "wisdom," accompanied by supernatural strength. (cf. Jude 20; Jas. 1:5; Phil. 4:13) This will go a long way in preventing and overcoming depression.

The battle is in the mind, for sure, and Satan will do whatever he can to side-track our thinking process. (cf. 1Pet. 5:7ff) But as stated above, we have a "renewed mind" and "greater is He that is in us, than he that is in the world (Satan)" We have a "helmet of salvation" in Christ which we must "put on" by faith, thus quenching every fiery missile (dart) thrown by the enemy. That's why we must deal with (confess) any resentment, bitterness, anger, unbelief, etc., so as to deny Satan any further inroad into our lives.

Let us consider some additional factors that may help in breaking through the darkness of depression.

Chapter Fourteen

Rehearsing God's Sovereignty

Let us first acknowledge that God is God over all! *"The LORD God omnipotent reigneth!"* (Revelation 19:6) Indeed, He is the "King of kings, and LORD of Lords!" Do we really believe this or not? Isn't this fact the basis of Romans 8:28-29, which most depressed people despise? Don't we "know that all things work together for good to them that love God" and are *"called according to His purpose?" "Shall not the Judge of all the earth do right?"* (Genesis 18:25)

After all, God is on the Throne of the universe–in absolute control of everything, seen and unseen. Does that "everything" not include us? How could we think otherwise? Since we *are* under His infinite watch care, then what's our problem? It is right at this juncture that we must be convinced that "God is good," working out everything in the believer's life for our benefit and His glory. It doesn't say "all things are good," but somehow through His power, plan, and time the "all things" become profitable—even our bouts with depression!

It is really upon this basis that we can forgive those who have deeply hurt us. For not only do all "things" work together for good, but all people as well. How else do you explain a Judas in the life of Christ? How do you reconcile this devilish betrayal with the love that Jesus manifested toward him? He surrendered it all to the Father—that's all we can do. Thus, we can freely "forgive those who trespass against us," knowing that our all-knowing Father has allowed the situation. Plus, He says: "Vengeance is Mine...I will repay!" It becomes His burden, not ours.

Remember grandma's special cake that looked and tasted so good? Watching it in the making, however, was not very appetizing. Check the ingredients which she dumped individually into the bowl; flour, egg whites, vanilla, salt, butter, and the like. To eat a spoonful of that mess could easily make you throw up. Yet, somehow she could whip it all up, place it in the cake pan and then in the oven, where a miracle happened. Under the right temperature and time, something delicious emerged that was scrumptious—especially after the whipped cream was applied!

So the ingredients of our lives are "whipped" together and properly "cooked" under the auspices of our faithful Heavenly Father. I grant you that this is a matter of faith in the unchangeable character of our God's goodness, but to whom else can we possibly turn? Who else can we trust to care for and control the intricacies of our lives? Indeed, "He is the First and the Last, the Beginning and the End"—and Everything in between! With a heart of surrender and praise, throw yourself upon Him, my friend, and find His grace all-sufficient in this present struggle! Let us cry out with the hymn writer:

> "Come, Thou Fount of every blessing, Tune my heart to sing Thy grace; Streams of mercy, never ceasing, Call for songs of loudest praise. Teach me some melodious sonnet, Sung by flaming tongues above; Praise the mount—I'm fixed upon it—Mount of Thy redeeming love. O, to grace how great a debtor, Daily I'm constrained to be! Let Thy goodness, like a fetter (chain), Bind my wandering heart to Thee; Prone to wander, Lord, I feel it, Prone to leave the God I love; Here's my heart, O take and seal it; Seal it for Thy courts above. Amen."
>
> —Robert Robinson

Chapter Fifteen

Understanding God's Purposes for Trial

No one will deny that life is stressful. But can we use that fact to excuse our defeat and discouragement? I think not. Are the trials of life geared to break us, or make us? I've heard it said that some new converts didn't grow in grace because of stressful circumstances, that is, when difficulties and trials came, they got discouraged and quit God. That scenario just doesn't line up with the Scripture, for trials are part of God's spiritual development program. Hardships are not geared to break us, but to make us!

It's a great day when the believer understands the true purpose of trials and that the results are positive and not negative. We are either victims or victors, depending upon how we respond. A large part of walking by faith is seeing life from God's vantage point, rather than our myopic or near-sighted perspective. We must resist the temptation of judging the Bible by what we experience, rather than judging our experience by the Bible. God's Word is the standard, not our feelings.

How to live for God when "the ducks don't line up" is a key consideration. This is where discouragement and depression develop when things don't go as we anticipated. Thus, it is imperative that we consider some of the Lord's purposes in sending trials and difficulties our way. Let me mention five:

1. To develop patience or endurance.
2. To validate our sonship.
3. To generate fervent worship.
4. To equip us for ministry to others.
5. To promote Christ-likeness.

Anyone interested? You mean that God is using these "depressing" circumstances to make me more like Him? Are you saying that this horrible darkness I'm experiencing can actually be used to make me a more effective servant? Yes, indeed! And the sooner we acknowledge and embrace these purposes with clarity and faith, the sooner we shall be delivered from the "fetal position"!

Trials Develop Patience and Endurance.

It is significant that in almost every sport, physical endurance is a key factor. A runner, for example, must aggressively train to go the distance without faltering. This takes a process of rigorous exercise geared to develop endurance. His ability to finish the race has everything to do with how well he has disciplined himself. No pain, no gain, as they say; withstanding the hardships in training somehow pay great dividends at the finish line.

So the believer is exhorted to *"run with patience the race that is set before us, looking unto Jesus..."* (Hebrews 12:1). With our focus upon Him, we can endure the trials. Since He is our Hope, our hearts can be encouraged when the race is most difficult. It is indeed a matter of perspective, i.e. understanding who God is and how He develops His children in the Faith.

In his letter, James challenges persecuted believers to respond properly to trials:

> *"My brethren, count it all joy when ye fall into divers temptations; knowing this, that the trying of your faith worketh patience. But let patience have her perfect work, that ye may be perfect and entire, wanting nothing." (1:2-4)*

CHAPTER 15: UNDERSTANDING GOD'S PURPOSES FOR TRIAL

Addressing them as "brethren" must not be taken lightly. This term refers, not to the unconverted, but to Christians who by the Holy Spirit's power could fulfill the apostle's challenge. Let's consider these words in light of our present discussion.

What does it mean to "count it all joy when you fall into divers temptations (many trials)?" You mean we should get excited—jumping up and down with shouts of praise? Well, not exactly. The word "count" here is a bookkeeping term for "accounting," thus, it means to consider or reckon this trial as joy in light of God's character and purpose. The hardship may bring tears, but faith can enable us to count it joy in our hearts. Why is this? Because we know that these trials of faith are "working (producing) patience or endurance."

The things we think are "killing" us are really making us! When we begin to understand this spiritual fitness program, we can actually "glory in tribulations!" (Romans 5:3) So James says to let patience do her perfecting work, that you might be fully mature, lacking nothing. O, to perceive this truth when we're tempted to collapse under stressful circumstances!

God can even use the "wrath of men to praise Him." Consider the early disciples, who when threatened by the religious rulers, gathered in one accord and countered the persecution with prayerful worship. Note Luke's narrative in Acts 4:23-31:

> *"And being let go, they went to their own company, and reported all that the chief priests...had said unto them. And when they heard that, they lifted up their voice to God with one accord, and said, Lord, thou art God, which hast made heaven and earth, and the sea and all that in them is: Who*

> *by... thy servant David hast said, Why did the heathen rage, and the people imagine vain things? ....And now, Lord, behold their threatenings; and grant unto thy servants, that with all boldness they may speak thy word....And when they had prayed, the place was shaken where they were assembled together; and they were all filled with the Holy Ghost, and they spake the Word of God with boldness."*

I purposely quoted this lengthy passage <u>first</u> to demonstrate the gracious victory given these disciples in the midst of persecution and severe trial. <u>Secondly,</u> it illustrates their endurance and determination to glorify God, rather than complaining or moaning about their suffering. They were on the divine offense, not defense. They saw the big picture rather than the difficulties close up. Their hearts witnessed the fact that it was all about **Him**, not about them! <u>Thirdly,</u> this episode in the early church may well be a preview of coming events in light of the militant Muslim jihad and other "politically correct" forces determined to stamp out vibrant Christianity. New believers in third-world countries are suffering intense persecution for their faith—some even murdered. In whatever form, this world is not a friend to grace, and we had better brace ourselves for the worst. The Christians in James' day were exhorted to "count it all joy" when subject to the fiery trials and to let patience do its work that they might be perfected.

Is this not a challenge for us today, my friend? God is maturing His children and, whether we like it or not, He has chosen to use trials in the process. Blessed is the saint who willingly submits to this training program—knowing in his heart that the trying of his faith produces endurance! This understanding will go a long way in bringing one out of the darkness of depression.

CHAPTER 15: UNDERSTANDING GOD'S PURPOSES FOR TRIAL

Trials Validate our Sonship.

God doesn't "spank" the Devil's children! He only disciplines His own. *"For whom the Lord loveth he chasteneth, and scourgeth every son whom he receiveth."* (Hebrews 12:6) What a tough, but comforting revelation this is! The Lord's training program is evidence that we belong to Him. He deals with us "as with sons"—we are uniquely His children.

> *"For what son is he whom the father chasteneth not? But if ye be without chastisement, whereof all are partakers, then are ye bastards, and not sons." (vs.7-8)*

The writer of Hebrews makes a strong case for the reality and verification of being a child of God. The very fact of being subject to "trial training" indicates the faithful love of our Heavenly Father. The absence of such trial and discipline renders one "illegitimate"—not a member of the covenant family. Concerned fathers deal with their children, how much more our Father in Heaven!

The very things that we may consider unfair, or at least unnecessary, are in reality an assuring witness that we are God's children. Not only that, but we can bank on the fact that, unlike many earthly fathers, His motives are always right. For they *"chastened us after their own pleasure; but he for our profit, that we might be partakers of his holiness."* (12:10) God has a higher and longer (eternal) purpose in His training than do fathers in the flesh who are limited by their own frailty and short-sightedness.

The writer is also quick to say that God's discipline is not joyous, but sorrowful; yet when it's over, there is a great yield of profit—*"the peaceable fruit of righteousness."* (vs. 11) As children of God, we rejoice in tribulation, realizing that we are being educated by our loving Father, who only does that which will glorify Himself and promote our good. There are no mistakes with Him. Thus we can rest as little children, putting our whole weight down upon His bosom. It behooves us to act like sons!

Trials Generate Fervent Worship.

We live in a generation of self-seekers and pill-poppers who act like the world revolves around them. Unfortunately, the church has been invaded with the same mentality. "Whatever makes you happy" is the theme song even among Christians. I'm convinced that the so-called "praise and worship" emphasis has deteriorated into a "feel good" experience. Without Spirit-anointed, solid expositional preaching of the whole counsel of God, worship is frivolous at best. It seems that there's much talk about worship without much evidence of a worshipful life. Could it be that we are worshiping "worship" rather than the LORD of Glory Himself? How else, for instance, can we explain the epidemic divorce rate among professing Christians?

Trials can be used to determine the genuineness of our faith. They can also serve to burn away the dross of carnality in our lives. Right response to tribulation can actually draw us closer to the Lord, inspiring a renewed confidence within. The great Apostle explains it this way:

> *"Therefore being justified by faith, we have peace with God through our Lord Jesus Christ: By whom also we have access by faith into this grace wherein we stand, and rejoice in hope of the glory of God. And not only [so], but we glory in tribulations also: knowing that tribulation worketh patience; And patience, experience; and experience,*

CHAPTER 15: UNDERSTANDING GOD'S PURPOSES FOR TRIAL

> *hope: And hope maketh not ashamed; because the love of God is shed abroad in our hearts by the Holy Ghost which is given unto us." (Romans 5:1-5)*

The key to persevering grace in trial is to understand our position in Christ. Paul expounds here the wonderful results of "being justified by faith," i.e., declared righteous in God's sight. Briefly stated, because of who Christ is and what He has done (the Cross-work), the believer is seen as sinless before the Father! None is righteous (Romans 3:10), but in Christ, one is dressed in His robe of righteousness. Glory! We are "justified" in Him—just-as-if-I-died! This is too good to be true, but it is!

As a result, we have "peace with God" (reconciliation); we have "access" to God Himself, and thus are filled with rejoicing hope which insures a glorious future in Christ. Wow! What a foundation and impetus to worship the true and living God! But this kind of faith and understanding is essential in order to face victoriously the trials that are up ahead.

It is great to revel in the riches of God's grace, but that really can't be done for long without the trials of life. Paul goes on to say that we not only "rejoice in hope," but we "glory in tribulations also." He really can't be serious, can he? How is it possible to welcome great difficulties and trouble without getting stressed out and discouraged? The answer is centered in our perspective of faith in the character and purposes of God.

The secret is "knowing (perceiving, being aware of) that tribulation worketh (literally, produces) patience (or endurance)." Here's the same truth that we discussed previously from James. In the midst of trials, it is what we know and understand about God that makes all the difference. What we think is what we are, and thus what we do. This is not the so-called "power of positive thinking" or the "name it, claim it" theology. It is rather the power and authority of redemptive thinking, resulting from true saving faith in Christ!

The benefits of such faith are astounding. This patience or endurance developing from trial in turn produces "experience," the word means "proof or tried character." It is translated "trial" in 2 Corinthians 8:2 where Paul commends those who in a great trial of affliction abounded in the freedom of giving. How could those who were poverty stricken give so liberally? Why weren't they depressed and resentful because of their lack of material substance? Why? Because of their "experience" of faith—that unswerving confidence or proof of Christ's all-sufficiency!

But that's not all. This ongoing experience of God's trustworthiness in trial also produces hope which in turn *"maketh not ashamed."* (vs. 5) I can't think of any quality more important in warding off depression than hope. As briefly discussed above, hope is that calm assurance and conviction that the LORD reigns supremely; thus, all things are and will be well.

I remember distinctly an experience that happened some twenty-five years ago while a pastor in New Jersey. I was going through a difficult time which was evidenced in my morning sermon. Following the service, a man visiting from Virginia approached me at the door. As he shook my hand, he commented on the message and then asked if I were having a tough time personally. When I acknowledged my struggle, he held up his Bible and shared the following word: "I just recently read the last chapter of this Book," he said, "and WE WIN!"

How encouraging was that statement. Yes, we may lose some battles along the way, but the war has been won! This fact should foster renewed faith and love in our spirit by which

CHAPTER 15: UNDERSTANDING GOD'S PURPOSES FOR TRIAL

we can effectively and boldly reach out for sinners and saints alike. Indeed, hope is the cement which holds faith and love together. Take away hope, and there is a waning effect on our faith and love.

In Philadelphia there's a book shop called "Who Dunnit." It stocks primarily murder mysteries and the like. I have never been a mystery "buff" per se, but if I were, this is how I would approach the subject. First, I would read two or three chapters, getting the characters and story plot. Then I would skip down to the last chapter and find out "who dunnit." I would then commence to read the middle chapters and revel in the fact that I know the outcome, while other readers are still puzzled about "who dunnit."

You say, "That would spoil the suspense of the mystery." To which I reply, "You've got a point, but look at how much fun I'm having in knowing the conclusion before it happens!" So it is with the Bible. How mysterious and puzzling is so much of its content. Even with the illumination of the Holy Spirit, our understanding can only scratch the surface at best. How are we to delve into the depths of its mysteries?

One possibility is to start in the beginning with Genesis, getting the foundation of creation and God's program in earth. Continue to read the ongoing saga of redemptive history, keenly observing the cast of characters and events. Then you might turn to the last book of the Bible and commence reading "the Revelation of Jesus Christ." The last chapter makes it clear that the War against Satan and sin has been won!

I can now read the remainder of the Bible with new and joyous understanding, because I know "Who Dunnit!" The Lord Jesus came the first time to deliver His people from the penalty and power of sin; the second time He comes, He will judge and destroy the ungodly. Satan will be eternally defeated and condemned. This conclusive knowledge sure helps me in this present walk of faith because I'm already on the winning side! We are "more than conquerors" because our "hope is in the Lord!" Faith and love can work effectively because "hope maketh not ashamed." Christ "in you, the Hope of Glory," insures such boldness! AMEN!

Trials Equip Us for Ministry to Others.

We've all heard the statement: "It takes one to know one." How difficult it is to really help someone in a horrendous circumstance through which we've never passed. It's hard to place yourself in someone else's shoes. On the other hand, what satisfaction comes when we are called upon to draw alongside a friend with whose difficulty we can identify. I have witnessed the great effectiveness of ministry to others by those who have suffered themselves.

I'm reminded of a situation years ago when a well-respected couple had lost their first child at birth. Very few attempted to minister to them directly, even though they tried to express their sympathy. It so happened that friends of mine had lost their firstborn just months prior to this couple. These friends had gone through tremendous grief, but God had demonstrated His great grace in their lives.

Hearing of this now-grieving couple, they were burdened to visit them and share their personal testimony of God's faithfulness in suffering. Needless to say, the Lord used those words of empathy from my friends to lift this couple's heavy burden. In fact, both couples were mutually blessed and edified, witnessing the hand of God that brought them together because of deep trial.

Is this not the very issue addressed by Paul in 2 Corinthians 1:3-4?

CHAPTER 15: UNDERSTANDING GOD'S PURPOSES FOR TRIAL

> *"Blessed be God, even the Father of our Lord Jesus Christ, the Father of mercies, and the God of all comfort; who comforteth us in all our tribulation, that we may be able to comfort them which are in any trouble, by the comfort wherewith we ourselves are comforted of God."*

One of the choice factors of being a Christian is to experience God's comforting peace in trying times. Here the Lord is called *"the God of all comfort"* who is well able to comfort His children in all kinds of tribulation. He's not the God of "some" comfort—but "ALL!" There is no situation too severe that can prevent the invasion of divine comfort and peace. In fact, Paul said in Philippians 4:6-7, that if we would cast our burdens before the Lord in prayer we would be secured by *"the peace of God which passeth all understanding."*

This kind of peace defies comprehension and explanation. Have you ever been in a devastating situation which seemed hopeless and yet you had a deep peace which you couldn't account for? You should have been "climbing the walls" or biting your fingernails, and yet an all-sufficient comfort engulfed your heart! That's the God of all comfort in operation.

I should mention that the word for "comfort" here is used of the Holy Spirit, promised by Jesus to be the "Comforter" of the saints (John 14:16). He is called the Paraclete, or "one called alongside" to console the believer. Yes, we have an Advocate—an Attorney who pleads our case before the Father! We have not been left comfortless (literally, "orphans"), but we are held to His bosom in the midst of the fiery trials.

The offshoot of this is the privilege to minister this comforting grace to others in trouble. How? It's accomplished through the overflow of the comfort which we have received from the God of all comfort (2 Corinthians 1:4). The very thing you may be going through now is actually preparing you to reach out to those whom God will place in your path. He's equipping us to identify with them. Indeed, "it takes one to know one." Therefore, we do not suffer in vain—there's always a God-given purpose. That thought alone is comforting.

Trials Promote Christ-likeness.

I would be remiss if I didn't include the glorious purpose that overrides all the others: Entering into the likeness of Christ or being "conformed to His image." You might be asking: "Why is God allowing me to go through this painful and difficult experience—it just doesn't seem fair?" Well, we might first reiterate that God is working out something good for Him and for you (Romans 8:28). But secondly, there has never been anything as unfair as the ignominious death of the Perfect Son of God. So whatever you are going through, one thing for sure, you can never suffer as Jesus did!

Yet there's a somewhat mysterious purpose of God for us as believers, i.e., entering into the sufferings of Christ. Paul expresses this spiritual quest when he testifies:

> *"...I count all things but loss for the excellency of the knowledge of Christ Jesus my Lord; for whom I have suffered the loss of all things, and do count them but dung, that I may win Christ."(Philippians 3:8)*

His education and legalistic religion were not able to save him; he traded in all his "religious junk" (worldly prestige, and self-righteousness) for the righteousness of Christ! Therefore, having been saved by the grace of God, he further cries out: O, *"that I may know him, and the power of his resurrection, and the fellowship of his sufferings, being made conformable unto his death"* (3:10). What is this all about? You mean to tell me that Paul didn't *know* him after all these years of ministry? Yes, but he had a longing to know Him in greater intimacy.

How then is that experiential knowledge fostered? Certainly we would all enjoy knowing "the power of his resurrection," but the apostle knew that such was impossible without entering into his suffering and death. This conviction is so foreign to our modern, worldly concept of Christianity! We will avoid hardship and suffering at any cost. In fact, anything other than "health and wealth" is considered taboo. No wonder we don't know much about resurrection power in these days!

Mental and spiritual toughness is a primary antidote for depression. Peter said,

> Be sober; be vigilant; because your adversary the devil, as a roaring lion, walketh about, seeking whom he may devour: Whom resist stedfast in the faith."
> (1 Peter 5:8-9)

There's a fight for our soul going on here and we must conquer the enemy by faith in Christ's victory!

In this connection, the apostle John makes a vital and significant observation regarding those who overcome the power of Satan. In Revelation 12:11, he mentions three avenues of victory: 1) the blood of the lamb, namely, what Christ accomplished for them at the Cross. 2) the word of their testimony, i.e., verbally confronting the enemy with their Spirit-filled position in Christ. 3) their total abandonment to the Saviour, without fear of death. Specifically it says, *"they loved not their lives unto the death."* Sold out to God! What a testimony!

I'm convinced that this is the stalwart attitude that must be manifested in the believer, not just toward greed, lust, drunkenness and the like, but in regard to the sin of unbelief. We must seriously determine to stand for Christ at any cost while refusing to give in to the world, the flesh, and the Devil!

Some time ago I was given a printed account of an African pastor who was martyred by rebels when he refused to renounce his faith. His testimony vividly and powerfully illustrates that sold-out, fearless love for Christ. The night before his death, he wrote the following lines on a scrap of paper:

HIS DISCIPLE

"I am part of the 'Fellowship of the Unashamed.' I have Holy Spirit power. The die has been cast. I've stepped over the line. The decision has been made. I am a disciple of His. I won't look back, let up, slow down, back away, or be still. My past is redeemed, my present makes sense, and my future is secure. I am finished and done with low living, sight-walking, small plan-ning, smooth knees, colorless dreams, tame visions, mundane talking, chintzy giving, and dwarfed goals!

I no longer need preeminence, prosperity, position, promotions, plaudits, or popularity. I don't have to be right, first, tops, recognized, praised, regarded, or rewarded. I now live by presence, lean by faith, love by patience, lift by prayer, and labor by power. My face is set, my gait is fast, my goal is heaven, my road is narrow, my way is rough, my companions few, my Guide reliable, my mission clear. I cannot be bought,

CHAPTER 15: UNDERSTANDING GOD'S PURPOSES FOR TRIAL

compromised, detoured, lured away, turned back, diluted, or delayed. I will not flinch in the face of sacrifice, hesitate in the presence of adversity, negotiate at the table of the enemy, ponder at the pool of popularity, or meander in the maze of mediocrity. I won't give up, shut up, let up, or burn up until I've preached up, prayed up, paid up, stored up, and stayed up for the cause of Christ.

I am a disciple of Jesus. I must go until He comes, give until I drop, preach until all know, and work until He stops. And when He comes to get His own, He'll have no problem recognizing me. My colors will be clear.

Lord, develop in me the perseverance and faithfulness to pursue Your goal for my life, even in the face of rejection."

-----Selected

My friend, the very thing you may be experiencing in your depression is the thing that is making you more like Christ. That which you think is "killing" you, **is**—so that He might increase, while you decrease! God has fixed it so that there is no spiritual gain without pain. Paul understood that concept, and what a great day it would be if saints today could receive the same truth. The result upon the church and the world would be phenomenal.

The apostle takes this idea to another level when he enumerates his sufferings for Christ in light of present ministry and eternal reward:

"Always bearing about in the body the dying of the Lord Jesus, that the life also of Jesus might be made manifest in our body...So

then death worketh in us, but life in you...For which cause we faint not; but though our outward man perish, yet the inward man is renewed day by day. For our light affliction, which is but for a moment, worketh for us a far more exceeding and eternal weight of glory." (1 Corinthians 4:10,12,16,17)

Paul saw the larger picture; he projected his suffering in light of eternity. So must we! It's a matter of perspective—seeing the present against the backdrop of the future. My life is in His sovereign hand, therefore, ALL things are working together for my good and His glory! And one day I will experience the "eternal weight of glory." Indeed, "it will be worth it all when we see Jesus."

New Testament believers seemed to portray a radical, sold-out abandonment to Christ and His cause. The Holy Spirit's fullness produced courageous acts and bold speech! This is perceived as "normal" Christianity. Such a believer in our country would be considered "abnormal" because the spiritual climate of the church today is "subnormal." What a tragedy!

The soft, worldly approach to Christianity today has paid its toll. Anything but a life of ease and prosperity is considered "unspiritual." Certainly suffering and trial cannot be from the hand of a loving God, can they? Thus, in light of this reasoning, trials are rejected. This is a grave mistake which counters the Scriptures and the history of the church. Listen to one hymn writer's challenge to our modern thinking:

"Am I a soldier of the Cross, a follower of the Lamb? And shall I fear to own His cause, or blush to speak His name? Must I be carried to the skies, on flowery beds of ease. While others fought to

CHAPTER 15: UNDERSTANDING GOD'S PURPOSES FOR TRIAL

win the prize, and sailed thro' bloody seas? Are there no foes for me to face? Must I not stem the flood? Is this vile world a friend of grace, to help me on to God? Sure I must fight if I would reign; increase my courage, Lord; I'll bear the toil, endure the pain, supported by Thy word."

----Isaac Watts

Chapter Sixteen

Recognizing that No Problem Can Rob Your Joy OR RECOGNIZING YOUR IDENTITY IN CHRIST (Exchanged life?)

It must be said that a Christian is a unique person, to say the least. He's exhorted to "lose his life," that he may "gain it;" to humble himself, that he might be exalted; to give, that he might have; to suffer, that he may be comforted; to die, that he might live. At first it all sounds like double talk, but in reality this is the paradox of the believer in Christ.

These characteristics point to the fact that the saint of God has a reservoir of stored grace that's beyond him. It is called the "fruit of the Spirit," which includes overcoming love, joy, and peace given directly by the indwelling Holy Spirit (Galatians 5:22-23). This means that regardless of the circumstance or problem, there is all-sufficient grace (enablement) available to the believer.

That being true, I would add another paradox to the Christian's life: He is the only one who can be happy and miserable at the same time! Whether it be a stomach ache or a heart break, he can still have the peace and joy of God in his spirit. How can this be, you ask? Simply because the joy and victory in the circumstance is a gift from the Lord, rather than something mustered up by myself. It is God meeting me in my need, a supernatural undertaking that's beyond my capability.

Yes, I can be "down" in a miserable situation, but simultaneously I can be "up" in my spirit. Dear friend, whatever your present struggle may be, look to Jesus who supplies overcoming strength. If you are not a true believer in Christ, may I plead with you to receive Him today as your Lord and Saviour! He alone is the Key to every aspect of life, here and hereafter. He alone is "the Way, the Truth and the Life!" There's no one like Jesus, NO ONE!

Making Right Choices

One of the great miracles of the new birth is the liberation of the will. In Christ, we have the privilege of choosing to do right because of our new nature. We can now choose right because we are right with God! This truth must never be minimized nor forgotten.

Away with the concept that "the devil made me do it" or "the circumstances were such that I had no choice." Paul said, *"Let God be true, but every man a liar"* (including ourselves)! We are *"more than conquerors"* through Christ, which indicates victory over the situation even though we're still in it. The apostle could say from a Roman prison, *"Rejoice in the Lord alway, and again I say, Rejoice!"* How is that possible unless you see the big picture—the plan and purpose of our Faithful God?

Take the extreme case of David who addresses God in an almost blasphemous tone:

> "How long wilt thou forget me, O LORD? forever? How long wilt thou hide thy face from me?...How long shall mine enemy be exalted over me? (Psalm 13:1,2).

Can you imagine someone talking like this to God? Yet, how many of us can identify with David, even though we may have never said these words out loud? Isn't this the heart-cry of depression? Aren't you glad that David tells it like it is? That sure helps me.

But let's not linger here, because David does something

CHAPTER 16: RECOGNIZING YOUR IDENTITY IN CHRIST

phenomenal which quickly brings him out of the doldrums; he turns his focus upon the faithful character of God and away from himself. Amazingly, he "shifts gears" in the midst of his dilemma and concentrates on the bigger picture. He says in verses 3 and 4:

> *"Consider and hear me, O LORD, my God: lighten mine eyes, lest I sleep the sleep of death; lest mine enemy say, I have prevailed against him; and those that trouble me rejoice when I am moved."*

This illustrates a vital move in the deliverance from depression. David is primarily concerned about the testimony of the Lord in the face of his enemies. He cries out for special grace to stand firm in the crisis so that the Lord may be glorified as his (David's) Sustainer!

This is faith in action, rather than a continuance of self-pity and unbelief. Notice how quickly David comes through this bout with the forces of darkness; he makes a declaration and a choice:

> *"But I have trusted in thy mercy; my heart shall rejoice in thy salvation. I will sing unto the LORD, because he hath dealt bountifully with me"(13:5,6).*

David didn't try to reason or medicate his way out of his despair but faced the real issue head on! It became a matter of who God is and whether He is able to deliver those who trust Him. Notice how this king declares his "trust" and then chooses to "rejoice" in the Lord's "salvation" (deliverance).

If that's not enough, he further chooses to "sing unto the LORD," because of His abundant grace! How can this be?

How can a man be so depressed that he feels like God has utterly forsaken him, and then just a brief time later he is singing God's praises?

My friend, it has to be a matter of perspective—seeing God as bigger than the circumstance. Remember, God will not allow anything to befall us that He hasn't ordained and given grace to endure. This truth didn't necessarily prevent David from bouts with depression, but it sure brought him out in victory when he remembered. So it is with us. No circumstance must ever be allowed to rob our joy.

Some time ago I received a unique poem called "God's Promise," from which I gleaned courage, strength, and instruction. By use of the alphabet, it cleverly and succinctly addresses the challenge of daily living:

> **A**lthough things are not perfect
> **B**ecause of trial or pain
> **C**ontinue in thanksgiving
> **D**o not begin to blame
> **E**ven when the times are hard
> **F**ierce winds are bound to blow
> **G**od is forever able
> **H**old onto what you know
> **I**magine life without His love
> **J**oy would cease to be
> **K**eep thanking Him for all the things
> **L**ove imparts to thee
> **M**ove out of "Camp Complaining"
> **N**o weapon that is known

CHAPTER 16: RECOGNIZING YOUR IDENTITY IN CHRIST

On earth can yield the power
Praise can do alone
Quit looking at the future
Redeem the time at hand
Start every day with worship
To "thank" is a command
Until we see Him coming
Victoriously in the sky
We'll run the race with gratitude
Xalting God most high
Yes, there'll be good times and yes some will be bad, but...
Zion waits in glory...where none are ever sad!
-------Selected

Preoccupation with Living for God's Glory

Finally, I want to discuss the capstone of the remedy over depression: Living totally for the glory of God, i.e., that *He*, not we, might be magnified (made great) in the eyes of others. Paul exhorts us that, *"Whether therefore ye eat, or drink, or whatsoever ye do, do all to the glory of God."* (1 Corinthians 10:31) I take this to mean that in every aspect of life (personal, financial, work, play, etc.) we give others the clear impression that Christ is indeed our Lord!

God saves us, not just for our benefit, but for His glory—that He might be magnified. Thus, it's all about Him and not us. When we make it all about us and not Him, that's when we become preoccupied with our feelings, situation, and fleshly perspective. That can only lead to selfishness, frustration, and discouragement. If indeed God did save us "on purpose for a purpose," then we can experience His freedom from worry and fear. We can live *above* the circumstance, while *in* the circumstance, without being *under* the circumstance.

A choice illustration of this overcoming attitude is found in Philippians 1:20 and 21, where the imprisoned apostle testifies:

> *"According to my earnest expectation and my hope, that in nothing I shall be ashamed, but that with all boldness, as always, so now also Christ shall be magnified in my body, whether it be by life, or by death. For to me to live is Christ, and to die is gain."*

What a challenge to believers today who are caught up in their own little world! Paul was facing the guillotine in a Roman jail when he uttered these words. He was face to face with death, yet boldly stands undauntedly for Christ. Why was he not "depressed" about the whole situation? Was it not because of his "earnest expectation and hope," namely, his intense anticipation and confidence in the Lord's reigning and sustaining power? He certainly exudes a determined spirit that no matter the outcome, Christ would be exalted.

Some may respond saying, "Yes, that was true of Paul the apostle, but it doesn't hold true today." Let me remind you of the myriads of believers martyred in the early church and down throughout church history. The saints who suffered under Communism demonstrated repeatedly what it meant to live and, if needs be, die for the glory of God.

How do we explain the spiritual tenacity of some Russian pastors who were incarcerated for many years in Communist prisons? How could they be tortured and

CHAPTER 16: RECOGNIZING YOUR IDENTITY IN CHRIST

humiliated for extended periods of time and yet remain faithful to the Lord Jesus Christ? They had no Bibles, devotionals, videos, music tapes, and the like. In addition, many were subjected to loud speakers in the middle of the night, blaring out Communist propaganda. How was it possible to maintain their mental sanity, much more their spiritual integrity, in such horrendous circumstances?

I have been told that many of these brave men, upon their release, went right back to preaching the Word of God to their flocks. This is not to say that some did not faint along the way, but it is astounding that so many demonstrated stalwart courage and victory in the face of such overwhelming opposition. There has to be an explanation for this; whatever it was, we must come to grips with such reality, for our turn may soon come!

Jesus laid down a principle which grants understanding to such bravery, whether under persecution or in everyday life. In the context of exhorting the disciples to "lay up treasure in heaven," i.e., seeking to magnify the Lord, He spoke this word:

> *"The light of the body is the eye: if therefore thine eye be single, thy whole body shall be full of light. But if thine eye be evil, thy whole body shall be full of darkness..."* (Matthew 6:22, 23).

A clear understanding of this truth is fundamental in dealing with depression and other issues. What is the "eye" to which Jesus refers? Is it the physical eye? If so, how would this apply to a blind person whose eyes are dysfunctional? On another occasion, He made a similar analogy regarding the ear: *"He that hath an ear, let him hear what the Spirit saith..."* referring to something other than one's earlobe. Obviously, He was likewise speaking of the inner or spiritual ear of the heart.

This heart or spirit of the believer is the receptacle of spiritual understanding. Man, unlike animals, has a God-consciousness, or the capability to perceive God. In an unbeliever, this "eye" is shut and blind, thus, the "whole body is full of darkness." But when the Holy Spirit opens our eyes, the light shines forth and we are flooded with spiritual understanding (light).

This is exactly what happened in Luke 24 as Jesus walked on the Emmaus road with two men whose *"eyes were holden* (shut) *that they should not know him"* (24:16). These men walked and talked with Jesus but had no clue as to who He was! After a robust conversation where they displayed their ignorance, it says in verse 31 that *"their eyes were opened, and they knew him* (Jesus)*."* Something happened that made all the difference in seeing the Truth.

Later on, referring to the disciples, Luke says, *"Then opened he their understanding, that they might understand the scriptures."* (24:45) Here Jesus, who is the Light, opens their spiritual eyes and reveals His light! This is the factor that divides a believer from an unbeliever—the light of understanding in the heart, opened by the Holy Spirit.

But in light of our discussion, when the heart is filled with God's light, then the darkness cannot overcome it. Light is a positive force, while darkness is negative—the absence of light. As long as the light is on in the room, the darkness is hidden. By precept, therefore, the light of God's righteousness overcomes the dark power of sin. This is what kept those imprisoned Christians sane under Communistic tyranny.

However, there's one catch or condition to this concept. Jesus states it this way: *"If therefore thine eye be single, thy whole body shall be full of light."* Single-mindedness, i.e. a sold-out attitude and focus on God Himself, is the key. Paul

CHAPTER 16: RECOGNIZING YOUR IDENTITY IN CHRIST

said, *"This one thing I do, forgetting those things which are behind...I press toward the mark for the prize of the high calling of God in Christ Jesus"* (Philippians 3:13). He was single-minded, knowing the admonition of James regarding the "double-minded man who is unstable in all his ways."

Believers are not to be narrow-minded, but singly focused on the glory of God. Thus, Paul testifies, *"For to me to live is Christ and to die is gain."* Christianity was not some religious system tacked on to his life. Rather, Christ *was* his life, another way of saying, real life *equals* Christ! So it must be in your life and mine if we are to "walk in the light" and dispel the darkness of depression.

Recently someone introduced me to a book called *Don't Waste Your Life*.[26] I was both refreshed and challenged by the author's passion for the supremacy of God in all things. His message, in essence, is to live every aspect of our lives in such a way that Jesus Christ looks great! Our goal should be to magnify God—to reveal His greatness to a lost and dying world. That can happen only as "our bodies are full of light," fostered by a single "eye" focused on the Lord.

Is this not what Jesus meant when He said, *"Let your light so shine before men, that they may see your good works, and glorify your Father which is in Heaven"*? "Thy will be done in earth (us) as it is in Heaven," should be our foremost desire. Therefore, we must believe our sufficiency is of God and indeed, "I can do all things through Christ which strengtheneth me"—regardless of my present circumstance.

Can I say further, that only a believer can be happy and miserable at the same time. When an unbeliever hurts in one place, he hurts in all. But the single-minded Christian may have a stomach ache, a toothache, or a heartache, but can still experience the joy and peace of God in his spirit! How can that be? It is because joy is a fruit and gift from the Holy Spirit and does not originate from the believer. The Spirit operates within us regardless of how we may feel otherwise. What amazing grace this is!

Someone may challenge the thesis of this book, relegating it to wishful thinking or some kind of unrealistic "perfectionism." Granted, that apart from the grace of God, the whole concept of living for God's glory is a farce! But we are to "grow in the grace and knowledge of Jesus Christ," becoming increasingly conformed to His image. Yes, through God's pruning process, we can progress in fruit-bearing from thirty, sixty, to one hundred fold. Indeed, we *are* "more than conquerors" in Christ, and that translates to our daily battles with temptation—even doubt, discouragement, and depression!

EPILOGUE

A PERSONAL TESTIMONY

As we draw this book to a close, I want to share something personal regarding our subject. Having been in full time ministry for over forty-five years, I have had considerable experience in much of what we have discussed together. My personal life has been replete with trial, discouragements, depression, darkness, and fear. I wrestled with thoughts of quitting the ministry and walking away from my responsibilities. As a young pastor, during a time of despair and disillusionment, I seriously entertained thoughts of suicide.[27] I can only testify of God's delivering and keeping grace over all these years.

Just recently the Lord saw fit to call my 20-year-old grandson Justin home. He had an extended battle with cancer that finally took him out of this world to a far better place. On the surface, it seemed like such a tragic waste of a young life, unless you really knew Justin. From a little boy, he possessed a godly spirit. As a teenager, he manifested a Christ-likeness that was contagious. He epitomized the statement: "For to me to live is Christ and to die is gain."

How blessed and challenged I was to know this young man. His walk with the Lord was never perceived as some religious trapping or ritual, but rather his natural lifestyle. Worshiping God was like breathing—nothing put on. How refreshing and effective was his testimony, as Christ overflowed from within. Somehow depression eluded him. Even through horrendous suffering and then into the shadow of death, he was able to magnify the Lord, making Christ look Great! He reminded us of why we are here on earth, for however long. I learned that it's not how long we live, but *how* we live that matters. Justin lived here only twenty years but did not "waste his life." He magnified the Lord to the very end of his earthly journey and we all need to do the same.

I, for one, have been challenged and revived by Justin's testimony. Several years ago, my wife, Chris, and I were discussing the possibility of retiring and living at a slower pace. I made the "mistake" of speaking too loud in Justin's presence; for he was quick to retort, "Gramp, you don't mean retirement, you mean 'refirement' don't you?" That struck me like a bullet to the chest! I can't get that statement out of my mind, nor do I want to. By God's grace, I'm committed to the end, that "Christ may be magnified, whether by life or by death." Lord, don't let me waste my life–there's too much at stake!

My friend, let me remind you just one more time, it's all about Him, not you! Yes, even in your present circumstance, God is working out His purpose. Don't faint, or rebel, but endure this dark moment, knowing it will eventually work out for your good and God's glory! He is all-sufficient, regardless what the health professionals say. His "tranquilizing" peace is still available to those who "cast all their care upon Him!"

Still true today is this antidote to fear and depression: *"Thou wilt keep him in perfect peace,* (literally, "double peace, wholeness") *whose mind is stayed on thee, because he trusteth in thee"* (Isaiah 26:3). If you have never surrendered your life to Jesus Christ and received His forgiving grace, do bow your heart before Him now. He will meet you right where you are. He will lift your burden and dispel the darkness of your soul, replacing it with His peace, His light and the fullness of joy! Then begin reaching out for others who need to be rescued from the same dark chamber that once held you. Let God use you to touch someone else with this message of hope.

Endnotes

[1] Articles by Bob Murray, Ph.D., www.upliftprogram.com "Cures for Depression Epidemic" and "Depression Facts and Stats." 11/3/2007.

[2] Elizabeth Wurtzel, *Prozac Nation—Young and Depressed in America* (Riverheard, 1995), intro.

[3] See Jay E. Adams, *Competent to Counsel* (Presbyterian and Reformed Publishing Co., 1970). This book challenges and instructs Christian leaders as to their obligation and ability to counsel hurting people.

[4] D. Martyn Lloyd-Jones, *Spiritual Depression* (Grand Rapids: Eerdmans Publishers, 1965), intro.

[5] A godly person reminds one of God. Take God out of his life and he has no reason or purpose to live.

[6] The distance from Mt. Carmel to Beersheba was some 110 miles—quite a jog!

[7] *Charisma News Service*, Vol. 2, No. 249, 2/26/01. These figures have been further inflated, seeing that some 7 years have elapsed since that study.

[8] SunScape Retreat Ministries, www.sonsscape.org ; Nov. 3, 2007.

[9] See Jer. 32:27-44, where God's people are judged and then mercifully delivered: "And they shall be my people, and I will be their God." (vs.38) Jeremiah even purchases a piece of real estate in anticipation of their return to the land (32:9).

[10] See writer's booklet, *Forgiven to Forgive* (Asheville: Revival Literature, 1995) for more insight on the cancer of bitterness.

[11] See 1Thess. 1:3, where these young believers demonstrated a working faith and laboring love because of enduring hope. Hope can be likened to the cement which holds faith and love together. Take away hope, and watch faith and love weaken, leading to depression. More on this subject will be discussed later.

[12] Asaph was the leader of all the music ministry in the Lord's

house; see 1Chron.6:31,32,39; 16;5.

[13] Sin began with Lucifer (Ezek.28:15) who was then expelled from Heaven. He became Satan, the deceiver, approaching the first couple in Gen.3. For further study on Satan's origin, consider Isa.14:12ff and Ezek.28:11ff.

[14] Note Jesus' own commentary on man's corrupt heart in Mk.7:14-23. It's not what goes into a man that defiles him (i.e. food, drugs, etc.), but what comes out of his heart. Every conceivable sin is already within man's fallen nature (see Jer.17:9); thus the need to be saved from the inside out, i.e. a new heart (e.g. the new birth, Jno.3:3; 2Cor.5:17). Religion always tries to reform a person from the outside in; but true salvation transforms a person from the inside out.

[15] See my booklet *Forgiven to Forgive* for further insight on this subject.

[16] Dave Hunt in "the Berean Call Newsletter," July 1999. www.thebereancall.org

[17] For a discussion of man's God-given functions, see the author's book *Healing for the Mind* (Asheville: Revival Literature, 1983), p. 109.

[18] Check the following verses that describe the mind's condition and need: Rom.1:28; 8:7; 12:1; Eph.2:3; 4:17; Tit.1:15.

[19] Peter R. Breggin, M.D. and David Cohen, Ph.D. *Your Drug May Be Your Problem, How and Why to Stop Taking Psychiatric Medications* (Reading, MA: Perseus Books, 1999). p. 2. Check the Bibliography of this book for abundant resources on this subject. See also Dr. Breggin's book called, *Talking Back to Prozac*.

[20] Idem.

[21] Alan Inglis, M.D. in "House Calls," February 7, 2008. www.healthrevelations.com.

[22] Ibid. p. 3.

[23] Ibid. p. 6.

[24] Ibid. p. 7.

[25] Idem.

ENDNOTES

[26] John Piper, *Don't Waste Your Life* (Wheaton, IL: Crossway Books, 2003).

[27] For further insights in mental and spiritual warfare, see the writer's book, *Healing for the Mind* (Asheville: Revival Literature, 1983) Web Site: www.revivallit.org. See many other helpful materials at this address.

A Summation and Glossary of Terms

"Know thyself" was a motto used by Socrates to rebuke those who "ridiculously" attempted to know obscure or vague things before knowing themselves. The theory is that only as man knows himself can he begin to understand and/or reach out to others. This has been man's quest from his inception (Gen. 1:26, 27; 2:7). But self-hood is only possible by God's direct creation; animals lack this vital trait that makes men and women human beings (persons).

So-called *evolution* denies this Biblical concept, failing to properly distinguish man from animals. We have *not* simply "evolved" over millions of years to become, as some claim, "the highest form of the animal kingdom." We are "human beings" directly created by God! If that's not the case, then how did we really begin? Where are we going? Who are we *now*? Do we really have a Personal Identity? These considerations are most serious if we're to "tackle" the subject of Depression.

Psychologists have labored tirelessly to understand what makes man "tick," so to speak. With all of its "labels" of Schizophrenia, Bipolar, etc., we still don't really have a clue, so psychiatry has stepped in with its myriad of psychotropic (mind changer) meds to treat the symptoms, at best. No one can really "know himself or herself" apart from "knowing" the One who made him initially. This is where the Manufacturers' Manual (The Bible) comes into play.

In order to understand man (humans), it's imperative to know and study the One who made them. Modern psychology attempts to compare one human with another, trying to explore the reason for their behavioral patterns. But "psychology" by definition means "the study of the soul (*pseuchos*) or mind. A human being is more than a "hunk of protoplasm with arms and legs;" he or she has an inner soul which is separate from the physical brain. To define "Psychology" as simply "behavioral science," as universities do, is to miss the mark. The issue is why do people "behave" like they do and how can they change? Apart from God's "Blue-Print" for humanity (The Bible), the popular psychological approach becomes an exercise in futility.

Much confusion and ignorance surrounds the subject of *depression*. It appears that we are attempting to "treat" the symptoms of various forms of "depression" without delving into the "root" problem. This is a complex subject, to be sure, and I have no easy answers to bring "instant healing." However, we do need to consider the precepts of God's Word, out of which come "the issues of life." (Prov. 4:33)

As we intimated above, no one can truly understand how man functions apart from the God who made him (Gen. 2:7). The first man was made in God's image (outward) and likeness (inward), cf. Gen. 1:26,27; therefore, we desperately need Biblical instruction to discern God's purpose for mankind and how to get him "back on track" since the Fall (Gen. 3). We are really dealing here with an "identity crisis," which is definitely linked to depression.

Let's consider briefly some of the terms used relative to "depression."

Discouragement

Everyone gets the "blahs" or feels "down" at one time or another. Obviously things don't go "right" all the time, and it's easy to be upset or distressed with our station in life. As one has expressed it, discouragement is "dissatisfaction with the past, distaste for the present, and distrust of the future." (Wm. Ward) Even as believers, we can lose sight of the blessings of yesterday, becoming indifferent to present opportunities, and uncertain about the future. It's a part of our human imperfection. It can also be the result of spiritual "warfare" (attacks) upon our minds, especially when not focused on the Word of God.

Discouragement means literally to "lose courage" or confidence; it has to do with our perspective and/or focus regarding our circumstance. A negative reaction to a situation can dampen one's enthusiasm and spirit, and if unchecked, it can lead to depression. Scripture says, *"Be careful (anxious) for nothing; but in every thing by prayer...let your requests be made known unto God"* (Phil.4:6) If we're to be anxious for *nothing*, we must pray about *everything*! There's something about prayerfully dropping our burden on the Lord that makes all the difference. (cf. 1Pet. 5:7)

Disappointments are inevitable, but they can turn out to be "God's appointments." It says of King David, who faced insurmountable troubles, that he *"encouraged himself in the LORD his God"* (1Sam. 30:6). This same man could then boldly exhort his distressed people to *"Cast thy burden upon the LORD, and he shall sustain thee."* (Psa. 55:22) He was aware of the fact that the same God who forgave his sin would also bear (carry) his burdens. This is the "bottom line" of nipping depression in the bud. Indeed, prevention is much better than the cure.

Depression

We could say that "depression" is the next level of prolonged discouragement. The word means to be "pressed down" mentally, with corresponding signs of loss of energy, decreased motivation, and exhaustion. We have more recently relegated depression as a form of "mental illness," but we must ask, is mental illness the root or the fruit of depression? Could it be that extended "wrong or faulty thinking" can trigger mental disorder or dis-ease? Are we responsible for our thoughts or not? To simply relegate depression as "mental illness" per se is to erase any human responsibility, making it (depression) merely an "illness." This is a critical issue.

There's no question that depression can create physical and mental problems just as worry, for instance, can spark digestive troubles. But the source of this problem goes beyond the physical, seeing that we also have a soul and spirit. What we think reveals who we are and affects every part of our being. As the reader has probably observed in this discourse, psychotropic medication (i.e. meds for the mind) does not begin to address this monumental problem.

Some readers may accuse the writer of discussing this subject from a Biblical or "religious" basis, ignoring the "findings" of modern psychiatric medicine. Let me introduce you to an American psychiatrist, Karl Augustus Menninger (1893-1990), who shook his profession at the roots in his book, *Whatever Became of Sin?* In his 1973 hardback edition, he addresses his psychiatric colleagues ("seers and prophets") as follows:

> "In all of the laments...made by our seers and prophets, one misses any mention of 'sin,' a word which used to be a veritable watchword of prophets. It was a word once in everyone's mind but now rarely if ever heard. Does that mean that no sin is involved in all our troubles—sin with an 'I' in the middle? Is no one any longer guilty of anything? Guilty perhaps of a sin the could be repented of or atoned for?...Anxiety and depression we all acknowledge, and even vague guilt

A SUMMATION AND GLOSSARY

feelings, but has no one committed any sins? Where, indeed, did sin go? What became of it?" (Pg. 13)

Menninger explains, "'What WAS the sin that no longer exists?'...I have in mind behavior that violates the moral code or the individual conscience or both; behavior which pains or harms or destroys my neighbor---or me, myself." (Pg. 17) He goes on to express that sin must not just be relegated to law-breaking criminals and deviants. On a personal level, "there IS immorality; there IS unethical behavior; there IS wrongdoing. And I hope to show that there is usefulness in retaining the concept, and indeed the word, SIN, which now shows some signs of returning to public acceptance." (Pg. 46)

As we'll see, the label "mental illness," may be suspect and detrimental to those who suffer from depression. Dr. Menninger provides vital insight in tackling this epidemic problem. We have attempted to deal with these root issues in this book. Hopefully, the greatest accomplishment will be preventative in nature, along with an understanding of the onslaught of depression and how to cope with it.

There is much controversy even in the church as to the kinds of depression. Is all depression "clinical" or physically induced? What about "chemical imbalance?" Is that a cause or result of depression? Can trauma, disease, or surgery trigger depression? Such instances are undeniable; there are complexities involved here. Is depression just another "disease" as diabetes or heart trouble? Certainly we don't place any "guilt" or personal "indictment" upon a diabetic, but what about someone who constantly struggles with depression? Are they the same? The primary consideration here is how our mind (thinking process) affects our body and general well-being. We've attempted to address some of these concerns.

What about the mental and spiritual warfare experienced by Christian believers who are prone to depression? Is there really an enemy determined to defeat us and drive us insane? That's certainly Paul's take in Eph. 6:10ff where we're admonished to "put on the whole armour of God," especially the "helmet of salvation," protecting our minds from Satan's "fiery darts" (missals). While we may not prevent such attacks upon the mind, do we have any responsibility and/or strategy to "fight the good fight of faith"?

It's evident already that the subject of "depression" is vast and complex. In my experience, personally and academically, I've yet to find someone with a clear and consistent understanding of the subject. To be sure, Christ is the Answer as revealed in His Infallible Word! Let's take that challenge as we daily ponder the Scriptures which supply the wisdom and strength for everyday life. Let us faithfully apply the lessons we've learned so as to be "overcomers" rather than being "overcome." Hear the glorious exhortation of Paul to needy and confident believers in Rom. 8:35f:

> *"Who shall separate us from the love of Christ? shall tribulation, or distress, or persecution, or famine, or nakedness, or peril, or sword? ...Nay, in all these things we are more than conquerors through him that loved us."*

Disclaimer

This book is primarily addressed to the general problem of depression, approached from a Biblical perspective. As we have seen, there are several key examples in the Bible of those who suffered greatly with this trauma. I have basically limited my discourse to these, and in no way have I attempted to deal with extreme "clinical depression" or patients "institutionalized" in the "fetal position" (under heavy medication). My heart aches for such people and I wish I could wave a "magic wand" and reverse their malady, but I cannot. I can only speak from my own limited perspective and understanding in the attempt to help people *way before* they become a proverbial "basket case."

Burnout

The term "Burnout" has been used to describe an ever-increasing phenomenon in our society. It was first coined in the 1970s by the American psychologist Herbert Freudenberger to explain the consequences of severe stress among highly motivated professionals. He witnessed the problems associated with those, like doctors and nurses, who sacrificially gave themselves to help others, often ending up "burned out," i.e. exhausted, lethargic, and unable to deal with the situation. Obviously, the "burnout" syndrome has spread way beyond the professional care-givers to those of every walk of life who feel overworked.

Many relegate burnout to a lethargy that occurs when a worker is not in control of how he does his job, or working toward goals for which he has no interest. (e.g. boredom?) Could it be a result of a psychological "breakdown" caused by the inability to cope with prolonged job-related stress? It definitely seems work-related, whereby workers feel emotionally drained and fatigued. Problems look insurmountable and hopeless; it leads to an "I-don't-care" attitude which promotes laziness and sapped energy. This explains the growing number of people who just don't show up for work. They increasingly live by their emotions, rather than their wills (moral character).

Significantly, "burnout" has become epidemic, not only in the secular world, but in Christian ministry. Pastors, missionaries, etc. are leaving their posts in droves, citing their inability to cope with frustration, disillusionment, and pressure to be "successful." This phenomenon is particularly prevalent in Youth Ministry, according to Greg Stier, a Christian Post guest columnist. After over 25 years working with young people, he says that youth leaders "face a ton of pressure. Unrealistic parental expectations, teen apathy, stressed marriages, low pay, over-packed schedules, and under-appreciated efforts are all contributions to youth leader burnout." He further cites a Youth Ministry Report which reveals that "the average youth leader stays in their position for 3 years."

Anyone in serious Christian ministry can readily identify with Mr. Stier's observations. Whether working with young people or adults, the potential of "burnout" is the same. It would certainly be less problematic if we could just "preach the Word" in an empty room; but we must minister the Word to *people* who have all kinds of problems. Unfortunately, ministers have their own share of personal difficulties and limitations. Mr. Stier further relates the "one overreaching reason" for youth leader burnout; that most leaders "down deep inside are not convinced they are making a lasting difference" in those to whom they minister. His "remedy" is to engage youth in "a movement of Gospel Advancing, disciple-multiplying activists who are unleashed into their schools to reach their peers…"

While the above challenge is lofty and admirable, how can it be implemented? Shouldn't saved, Spirit-filled young people already be engaged in such activity? Are leaders facing the dilemma of trying to minister to those who are still unconverted, thus having no genuine spiritual interest? Trying to "Christianize" a group of "heathens" is tough work indeed, leading to rapid "burnout." Could we deduce here that burnout has many of the same factors related to "depression?" I think this correlation has already been expressed in the book. The Bible, thankfully, addresses these issues and answers and we

A SUMMATION AND GLOSSARY

have explored some godly examples of those who experienced the deep struggles of depression, granting us personal insight into this present-day dilemma.

Oppression

While depression seems to focus on "pressure" from within, oppression has reference to a downward pressure from an outside force. This is evident when reading about an "oppressed people" under a communist regime, for instance. People are held in sway, controlled by those in power. This is depression taken to another level of spiritual warfare or demonic influence. It's more than simply being mentally "defeated" or exhausted.

Jesus, in Acts 10:38, is described by Luke as One:

"anointed...with the Holy Ghost and with power; who went about doing good, and healing all that were oppressed of the devil..."

We know that Jesus did more than just "preach the Gospel," per se; He cast demons out of demonically-possessed people, who then hopefully became believers. (cf. Mk. 5:1-20) But possession and oppression are not the same. A true believer in Christ is indwelt by the Holy Spirit and thus cannot be "possessed" (indwelt) by Satan. However, a true believer can be attacked and influenced by demonic power in various ways. (e.g. "spirit of fear"-2 Tim.1:7). This is why Paul admonishes us to put on the "whole armour of God that we may stand against the wiles (strategies) of the Devil;" particularly, he mentions the "helmet of salvation" to protect our thought life. (c.f. Eph. 6:10ff; 1 Pet. 5:7f))

This is a vast subject which cannot be exhausted here. Suffice it to say that depression primarily deals with our past while oppression is concerned with the future. Looking back or focusing on the disappointments, injustices, hind-sight grievances of what "coulda, woulda, shoulda," been etc. can promote depression and bitterness. Paul's word is "don't let the sun go down on your wrath (anger)..." i.e. deal with resentment pronto, so as not to "give place to the Devil." (cf. Eph. 4:26, 27) To harbor anger toward others, including God Himself, is serious business which will affect a believer's mental and spiritual sanity!

To be preoccupied with the future is another serious problem. We're admonished to *"be careful* (anxious) *for nothing; but in every thing by prayer...with thanksgiving let your requests be made known unto God..."* (Phil. 4:6) The basis of worry is fear of the future. It robs us from living in the present and enjoying God's daily provision. This is a cleaver scheme of our Enemy, i.e. to tempt us to live either in the past or in the future, and thus robbing us of God's joyous tranquility for the present. Undoubtedly, this dilemma is one result of the Fall of Adam and Eve. (c.f. Gen. 3) Yesterday is gone, tomorrow is uncertain, and today is all we have; we need to make the most of it.

A Lesson from Wildlife

I've often been enamored with the ability of wildlife to be contented with the present. It must be said that, unlike sinful man, animals obey their Creator; that's why a fish is content in the water and likewise a cow giving milk. The birds feeding at my kitchen window seem so "unconcerned"—how can that be? Obviously, they are doing what they were created to do. This is why Jesus Christ came to die for man, the sinner, not animals (cf. Heb. 9:27). In addition, I believe that animals have a limited "thinking" ability, but they never think about what they think! That's how they live "in the present" and never need a "psychiatrist!"

A SUMMATION AND GLOSSARY

Humans, on the other hand, have a unique mind which not only "thinks," but thinks about what it thinks! This God-given capacity to ponder the past and explore the future can make the thinking process problematic. The ability to focus on the past and/or "dreaming" of the future can either "make us" or "break us," for as a man *"thinketh in his heart so is he."* (Prov. 23:7) We can't live any higher than we think. To be obsessed or constantly preoccupied with the hurtful events of the past can readily lead to depression. Likewise, to be obsessed with the future (unknown) will produce anxiety and open the door for oppression (abject, uncontrollable fear).

Animals in their innocency are able to live in the "now" (present). Sin spoiled that for mankind, who seems to have real difficulty enjoying the present tense. It is significant that The LORD revealed Himself to Moses as "I Am That I Am" (Jehovah), i.e. the God of the Eternal Present. (Ex. 3:14) That He is the Lord of the Eternal "Past" and "Future" is unquestionable. However, the emphasis here seems to be Eternal God as accessible to the believer in present circumstance—*"a very present help in trouble."* (Psa. 46:1)

John's Gospel bolsters this truth when he portrays Jesus seven times as the *"I Am,"* not "I was" (although He always "was" and ever "shall be!") For example, Jesus says, "I *am* the living bread…I *am* the water of life…I *am* the light…I *am* the way, etc." Thankfully, all of these attributes of Christ are applicable to the believer in the *present*. Amen! In light of this personal provision, I'm convinced that genuine mental health is hinged on the divine ability (grace) to live in the present tense, apart from any focus on past history or undo concern (worry) for the future.

Addendum

So-called "mental illness" can be relegated and

simplified by just two conditions: Psychosis and Neurosis. The former (Psychosis) applies to a person who has lost touch with reality (def. of "insanity"). He believes, for example, that 2+2 = 5, and thus cannot adjust to society. The latter condition (Neurosis; i.e. excessive anxiety) pertains to one who is sane; he agrees that 2+2 = 4, but it *bothers* him! This person lives in reality but is not handling it well. Thus, the potential for depression, etc.

Please don't hesitate to re-read the book in light of this entire section. My prayer is that the Lord will be pleased to use that endeavor to further generate understanding, edification, and healing grace in your life. Amen!

Selected Bibliography

Adams, Jay E., *Competent to Counsel.* Nutley: Presbyterian and Reformed Publishing Company, 1970.

Breggin, Peter R., and David Cohen, *Your Drug May Be Your Problem, How and Why to Stop Taking Psychiatric Medications.* Reading, MA: Perseus Books, 1999.

Bridges, Charles, *An Exposition of Proverbs.* Marshallton: The National Federation for Christian Education, 1846.

Brooks, Thomas, *Precious Remedies against Satan's Devices with the Covenant of Grace.* London: Sovereign Grace Publishers, 1676.

Finnigan, William J., *Forgiven to Forgive.* Asheville: Revival Literature, 1995.

_____ *Healing for the Mind.* Asheville: Revival Literature, 1983.

Lloyd-Jones, Martyn D., *Spiritual Depression—Its Causes and Cure.* Grand Rapids: William B. Eerdmans Publishing Company, 1965.

McMillen, S. I., *None of These Diseases.* Westwood: Fleming H. Revell Company, 1963.

Nee, Watchman, *The Spiritual Man.* 3 vols. New York: Christian Fellowship Publishers, Inc., 1968.

Piper, John, *Don't Waste Your Life.* Wheaton, IL: Crossway Books, 2003. Check www.desiringGod.org .

Solomon, Charles R., *Handbook to Happiness.* Wheaton, IL:

Tyndale House, 1982.

Stewart, James A., *Heaven's Throne Gift.* Asheville: Revival Literature, n.d. www.revivallit.org .
**

About the Author

Pastor, teacher, and presently Biblical instructor at the Discipleship Academy in Youngstown, Ohio, Bill Finnigan has been engaged in active ministry for over Fifty years.

A native of Newark, New Jersey, Bill received a call to ministry while in college. The ensuing years were spent in intensive study to learn and sharpen ministry skills. Attending several universities, he holds a number of degrees, including the Doctor of Ministry. For over twenty-seven years, Bill held pulpits in Pennsylvania and New Jersey, reaching people with God's life-changing Word.

His outreach experience has included radio, prison, and Bible conference ministries. He has served as a college professor, and director of a Biblical counseling center. He has authored other publications, including *Healing for the Mind*, offering comfort and remedy for mental turmoil, *Forgiven to Forgive*, which serves as an antidote to resentment and bitterness, and *Living Skillfully,* a commentary on Proverbs.

Along with his wife, Chris, Bill continues to be busily engaged in the Lord's work, considering himself "refired," rather than retired.

Dr. William J. Finnigan
8883 Sherwood Dr. NE
Warren, Ohio 44484
email:bilfinn1@yahoo.com

www.ingramcontent.com/pod-product-compliance
Lightning Source LLC
Chambersburg PA
CBHW071118090426
42736CB00012B/1946